SELLING SACRED GROUND

SELLING SACRED GROUND

*Will Real Estate
Agents Be Relevant
or Replaced?*

CRAIG FARESTVEIT

NEW YORK

LONDON • NASHVILLE • MELBOURNE • VANCOUVER

SELLING SACRED GROUND

Will Real Estate Agents Be Relevant or Replaced?

Published in New York, New York, by Morgan James Publishing. Morgan James is a trademark of Morgan James, LLC. www.MorganJamesPublishing.com

ISBN 9781642794632 paperback
ISBN 9781642794649 eBook
Library of Congress Control Number: 2019901294

Cover Design by:
Henry Artime and Bianca Mascorro

Interior Design by:
Christopher Kirk
www.GFSstudio.com

Morgan James is a proud partner of Habitat for Humanity Peninsula
and Greater Williamsburg. Partners in building since 2006.

Get involved today! Visit
MorganJamesPublishing.com/giving-back

For Andrea, who has always been the music of our life long dance together.

Thank you to Dr. Gunnar Lee-Miller and Paige Martini for all of the time you gave to me throughout this writing project. Thank you to Don, Jeremy, Henry, and Tom for your consistent encouragement. Thank you Bianca for all of your work on this project. Thank you to Caren, Ethan, and Kathy as well.

Thank you Ara, for all of these years working together.

Thank you to all my clients who have allowed me the humbling privilege of working with them.

Thank you to the many agents who have inspired me to do this job well. Just to name a few:

Brad, Gretchen, Ellie, Sandra C., Jon, Bonnie, Diana, Kathy, Gerri, Jeannie, Carey, Ben, Sylvie, Janice, Razmik, Harry, Pakrad, Margi, Keith, Kathy, Eric, Brit, Vince, Gillan, Reiko, Brent, Regina, Pam, Leah, Suzanne, Kay, Kevin, Beatrice, Kendyl, Dawn, Steven, Jennie, Sookie, Beverly, Ruth, Julie, Shirley, Gena, Chris, Sandra, Wes, Jill, Helen, Cheyenne, Liz, Anne, Arthur, Bert, Hamlet, and Tom

Table of Contents

Foreword

I've known Craig for more than 20 years and he's been a great friend. Among other things, we've played golf at St. Andrews in Scotland and done a tail hook landing on an aircraft carrier off the coast of California. We've laughed and cried together, and shared our successes and failures. We've held each other accountable and learned a lot from each other along the way. When my dad died in 2006, I naturally asked Craig to help us sell our family home, which my dad had built in 1948. There was one other house for sale in the neighborhood at the time, and it had been listed for three or four months, with little or no activity. When I sat down with Craig to talk about it, he described a very simple process that would result in a successful sale in a relatively short period of time. That process is the one Craig writes about in this book. It played out exactly the way he said it would, and we sold the house for more than the listing price within two weeks of the date it was first shown to potential buyers. I couldn't have asked for more. By the way, the other house in the neighborhood didn't sell for another two or three months. I assumed, because Craig was my friend, that he went above and beyond what he would normally do for a client. But, I soon realized that he does this for all his clients. He is truly an exceptional real estate broker. If you are looking for a blueprint for success in the real estate business, or are looking to buy or sell a home, this book is a must read. It can also be a blueprint for success in life and relationships. Craig brings the same commitment, deep caring, consistency and intention to everything he does. He's been a great role model for me and I'm grateful to have him in my life.

Don Riddell, Executive Coach

An Odd Norwegian Fable...

There once was a town full of people that loved apples. Or at least they really *liked* apples. More accurately, they loved their sprawling grove of plentiful apple trees. Over many years, the town had grown around this beautiful field of apple trees so that it seemed to belong equally to all of the townspeople. Unofficially, every citizen assumed a specific role in caring for the apple trees. Some seemed to enjoy the weeding and the trimming, while others were good at harvesting, and still others would take care of delivering the apples to market. It all just sort of happened "organically", as the newer town people were want to say. All enjoyed the beauty of the orchard and all shared in the bountiful crop of apples produced each year.

An informal "apple orchard guild" coalesced over the years into a group with two annual meetings: just prior to harvest, which became known as "The Picking", and "The Counting" just before winter . The members did make some money as the apples became sought after by apple lovers far and wide, but most of the proceeds went back into their beloved orchard.

As with most groups of people, different ideas were put forth and squabbles took place, but every year the trees were cared for and the apples grew. However, as the proceeds grew, so friction grew within the Apple Guild. Phrases such as "real money" and "arbitrage" started to boil within the apple loving community. The pressure became so great that one year the guild voted to delegate the harvesting and selling to the Mr. Apple Consortium. Mr. Apple himself made the winning presentation:

> *"My good people of Appleton, my team of experts and our efficient machines will harvest your field in one night and produce dazzling results. We harvest only at night for the darkness best preserves the taste of a just-picked apple."*

When harvesting night came, it was dark indeed. Mr. Apple's expert team and their miracle machines worked noisily all night with earth-shaking and ear-splitting efficiency. By morning the entire orchard was harvested. Every tree pulled up by the roots, every apple shaken from its tree, every tree cut into neat cords, and every apple crate stacked in long rows.

Mr. Apple met with the dumbstruck Guild and offered to sell them the entire crop of apples at three times the highest price ever paid- "Because these are the very last of the famously delicious Appleton apples," he explained.

"And what about our apple trees?" a long time member of the Guild shouted.

"Oh," Mr. Apple responded while looking down at his watch, "I have sold them all as firewood."

The Apple Guild gathered from every member a huge sum to pay Mr. Apple for that last crop, but they did not taste of one. Instead, they began carefully removing every precious seed and making plans for planting.

Introduction

There is an unprecedented and unrelenting attack on the integrity of the space in which we make the most important decisions in our lives.

We are all faced with important decisions every day. Remain in this career, or make a change? Enroll our child in public school or private? Continue chemotherapy for Mom or consider hospice care? And much of the time, our lives demand that we make these crucial decisions in fields where we are not experts.

Over the last several decades, we have gained unimaginable and immediate access to information that used to be the private domain of the experts in their given field. Travel, financial, and even medical information is no longer solely provided in consultation with a travel agent, a financial planner, or a doctor; the growth of companies like Expedia, Charles Schwab, and WebMD make it readily available to anyone with WiFi. Traditional experts in these fields are scrambling to adjust to

1

their changing roles in working with their clientele and more informed patients. But does our ability to use this information really match the growing access we enjoy to it?

The mounting pressure and sheer weight of information and/or choices available to us may be clogging our processing abilities. Dr. Barry Schwartz speaks eloquently to the paralysis of choice within an exponentially growing list of options in both his book *The Paradox of Choice* and his TED Talk of the same name. Dr. Schwartz is a college professor, and his observations on the struggles of contemporary college students particularly stand out to me. He explains that a college student of a specific major say, 20 years ago, had a handful of routes within that school to complete the requirements of that major. Now, his students have the freedom to select thousands of different customized routes to complete their majors, which seems wonderful as they learn to navigate their customized path through that educational system. What Dr. Schwartz has observed, though, is that these students are actually not as capable as their peers from years prior who had more defined paths through their majors, with the result that he has had to lessen the amount of work he gives to his current students by about 20%. By Dr. Schwartz's measure, this increase in choices for the student's consideration has decreased their capability. Clearly, the proliferation of choices is not serving them well.

You might be tempted to argue that this overabundance of choices is not inherently malign, but rather a more neutral problem that might be solved by better management. But there is evidence of bad intent within our growing world of information too. To make our choices well, we need a clear presentation of the facts, risks, and the options. What we fear is the self -interested leading of the expert on which we are dependent. We can all agree, for instance, that the selection of our political leaders is a choice that is important to us all, and therefore that our decisions in this arena are to be respected. We are accustomed to the heightened degree of advertising involved in a political campaign, so when we are deciding which candidate to consider for President of the United States, we can discern pretty well through the slogans and "promises" in our theater of politics to get the measure of the woman or man running for that office. But it is sobering to witness the lengths of algorithmic guile, à la Cambridge Analytica, that may have been a sophisticated attempt to manipulate that place where we exercise our right to vote. Whatever you think of the political consequences of such actions, we can agree that if such manipulation of data can be profitable in the marketplace, there will be those who seek to do so.

I do not want to be that Drunk Uncle at Thanksgiving dinner proclaiming, "The AI's are gonna control the gover'mint." Even sober, I do not have the right nor the ability to make any broad declarations about our culture or marketplaces. But I do have a unique standing and ability to speak to a small sliver of our marketplace that is both dear to us as well as threatened by the proliferation of choices and bad information: our homes.

I have been a very active residential real estate agent for thirty years. When I first started in real estate in 1988, we had two computers in an upstairs office serving two full floors of agents. We did not even use the computers to search for properties online, as those were still only available in large phone book style paperbacks that were distributed weekly to agents in our area. This now seems comical, as online real estate data organizers such as Redfin, Realtor.com, and Zillow can provide your neighbors and mine with a wealth of information in seconds : what we paid for our homes; how much in loans we have against it; what it is worth today; and more.

Residential real estate is a timely and illustrative example of what is occurring in our decision making in the midst of a glut of information. Ever since agents gave up their guild-like control of real estate data in the late 90's and that information became available online, the question has inevitably been posed, "How long will it be until the residential real estate agent will prove a redundant cog in the machinery of our purchase and sale of our homes?" The traditional residential real estate expert has provided specific training and experience to this important transaction on behalf of their clients, but at present, online data platforms like Rex are seeking to replace that traditional agent with the promise of lowering costs to the process of buying and selling a home- a transaction that takes place approximately 5 million times a year in the U.S. marketplace.

In our DIY culture, the bypassing of the traditional associated professional in exchange for hoped-for savings is quite compelling, especially when matched with the promise of direct access to all pertinent information. These real estate data sources are working feverishly to create a magic algorithm that best automates the rather old-fashioned model of buying and selling a home. They treat the process of residential real estate like a recipe; once they identify the ingredients for success, you too can follow the steps and whip up a successful sale or purchase of your home.

And therein lies the difficulty in doing so. We refer to these physical structures in which we live as something more, as a museum is more than a warehouse for art, and a temple more than a meeting hall for people of faith. We call these structures that we live in, these houses, our **homes.** Our homes are a place of intangible value, where we not only keep the most important things in our life, but where we care for the ones we hold most dear.

In this book I will place the role of the residential real agent under the microscope in hopes of determining the value, or lack thereof, that she/he/they actually provide for their clients within the purchase or sale of a home. To do so thoroughly, we will walk together through the details of the entire residential real estate transaction in depth. The payoff for this challenging stroll will be two-fold: we will define what this sliver of our marketplace actually does, and in so doing decide its future viability within our marketplace.

Now, a disclosure about limits. I remember vividly the daunting task of attempting to write a eulogy for my mother. I wanted it to be both authentic and true. I quickly realized that I could not tell my mother's story from either of my brothers' perspectives, nor my sister's. All I could do was tell that part of my mother's story that I had witnessed and knew to be true.

I have not sold a home in Seattle, New York, or the Florida Keys, but I am sure that each region has its own relevant details that must be investigated and managed during the sale of a residence there. Though details may be unique to a given area, the process of correctly managing all those details is analogous across the country. What I have done, and can speak to, is thirty years of work with home Buyers and Sellers in a dozen or so zip codes just northeast of Los Angeles. Whether our reflection on residential real estate proves as eulogy to my profession or not, we will find out together. Let's begin with an all-too-common story of a neighbor selling their cherished longtime home.

The Sad Tale of the Ascot's Sale

The Ascots love their longtime home. It is a two-story Spanish Revival home that was built in 1923 on a lot with a wonderful view overlooking the city. Their children have grown and moved away, and they think it might be time to downsize to a smaller one-story home. Their neighbor is a real estate agent; she has always seemed nice, and she works for a well-known company in town, so they arrange to meet with her. She confidently insists that their home is even more valuable than they had hoped. They list their property with her for $1,750,000. A week later a *For Sale* sign has been installed in their yard and they are on the market. It all seems to be happening so fast.

But time slows to a crawl as they host one open house after another. Their agent, Leslie, explains that "people love the house, but think there is too much work to do." This feedback at first surprises and then frustrates the Ascots, as they have often been told how beautiful their home is by friends and neighbors. After two months on the market, Leslie convinces them to lower their asking price by $75,000. More open houses follow and, finally, they receive a lower offer, with which they negotiate and settle at $1,625,000. All this while, Leslie has been showing the Ascots smaller homes and they end up falling in love with one. Though the home has several offers already, they offer well above the asking price and secure an accepted offer on their hoped for "forever" home.

Though the Ascots assumed that the Buyer of their current home would have the house inspected, they are alarmed to learn that the Buyer has scheduled *five* inspections: a general inspection, a foundation inspection, a chimney inspection, a sewer inspection, as well as that of a geologist. After the general inspection, they are informed by their agent that the Buyers, Mr. and Mrs. Castillo, have scheduled another two inspections, one by an electrical contractor and the other by a heating and air company.

Mr. Ascot begins to worry. Besides the obvious floor settlement in their breakfast room, the Ascots have never experienced serious issues with the house. Though the window in that breakfast room did not open any more, the view out of that old casement window was so lovely that it had never seemed to matter. The Ascots are honest people, and had of course relayed all this to Leslie during her first visit when she had asked if they had ever experienced any significant problems with the property. At that time, they had also recounted to Leslie that they added central heating and air upstairs back in the summer of '83. That HVAC work was completed by the same contractor, a family friend, who had added the guest quarters over the garage the year before so that their in-laws could enjoy a nice space whenever they visited from across the country.

Finally, the Castillos complete all of their various inspections. Soon after, Leslie calls the Ascots to ask to meet with them to review a letter she received from the Castillo's agent with regards to the inspections. When she arrives, her voice shakes as she insists that she "could not believe" that the Buyer's agent would have the audacity to submit such an aggressive request. All in all, she explains, the Buyers are asking for a price reduction of $100,325 and, on top of that, they want two additional items corrected. Attached to the letter from the Castillo's agent are various inspection reports and estimates from various contractors:

1. All's Well Foundation: Replace 37 linear feet of foundation on the view side of the house, as well as bolt the rest of the foundation: $17,000.

2. Tri-City Electric: Remove and replace all of the knob and tube wiring, upgrade outlets to three prongs, GFCI in the kitchen and bathrooms, and replace the main electrical panel with new 200-amp panel: $22,000.

3. Sewer Video and Repair: Replace 130 feet of original clay tile sewer from the back corner of the house out to the side walk, which is currently riddled with tree roots. Also, the 6-inch line under the street to the City sewer is damaged. Estimate to replace 130 feet of line while re-lining that section under the street: $23,000.

4. Mitchell Chimney and Masonry: The ornate double flue brick fireplace serving the living room and den has some cracks and will need to be re-built from the roofline up and the master bedroom fireplace flue needs

to be re-lined and that chimney braced in the attic: $14,000 and $8,700, respectively.

5. Noteworthy Central Heating and Air: The original gravity heater in the basement, which heats the ground floor, is shrouded in insulation containing asbestos, as are all the ducts. The heating and air that was added in the early 80's is far past its useful life expectancy and was probably installed without permits, as it was connected to the original asbestos insulated ducts that service the top floor. The cost to replace those old units, including asbestos remediation: $15,625.

Along with their request for a large price reduction, the Castillos requested two items for the Ascots to complete prior to the close of escrow: 1. Repair the cause of the natural gas smell near the gas meter, and 2. Complete the permit process for the guest quarters over the garage.

In regards to the gas leak, Leslie chirps "Not to worry" as she is sure that if the Ascots simply call the Gas Company, "they will check for a leak as a free service." But as for the guest house permits, the Ascots are baffled. Their friend was an active contractor back when that job was completed, and had had a very good reputation. They had asked that the addition be completed with proper permits and they clearly remember paying their contractor for the permit process – plans, engineering, inspections, etc. But along with the Buyer's written request, the Buyer's agent provided a copy of a permit from the 80's for the guest quarters over the garage clearly marked as "Expired."

The Ascots are quite upset. Leslie had assured them that the Castillo's offer was an "as-is" offer. Back when they had purchased the home over 40 years ago, they certainly remember having a contractor walk with them around the house, and, though it was not in perfect condition, they were willing to accept those imperfections as its seemed to be doing well for its age. It would never have occurred to them to ask the Seller to give them back some money or lower the purchase price. They had agreed to pay $225,000 then, and that is what they had paid. All of the issues the Castillos are raising seem, in their minds, just what any Buyer should expect when purchasing an older home. It is all a part of the very vintage character that makes the property so charming and so special.

The Ascots decide that these Buyers must be "trying something" and they consider cancelling escrow and selling the property to someone else. Leslie agrees that though it is customary for a Buyer these days to complete several inspections, these requests are "just ridiculous." But, she adds, as if as an afterthought, if the Ascots cancel the transaction with the Castillos, "we will still need to disclose all of these reports to any subsequent Buyer." Now Mr. Ascot is really mad and tells Leslie to "just cancel this deal".

Mrs. Ascot absolutely disagrees. Though she is also very upset with the Buyer, she really loves the little forever home that they are trying to purchase, and frets that it will be very difficult to find a smaller home like it in the exact neighborhood she had hoped to be in and still have a view. She has been attending open houses for the past year and realizes the rarity of the home they have in escrow.

They speak again by phone the next day and Leslie advises them to offer the Castillos half of what they are requesting, confidently adding "I know these kinds of Buyers." She is sure "they are just trying to re-negotiate the deal now that we are in escrow." Feeling betrayed by the Buyers and the situation, the Ascots relent and offer a $50,000 price reduction because of their desire to complete the purchase of their downsize home.

The Castillos, through their agent, respond with a firm "No". With the response from the Buyer's agent comes a long letter from the Castillos to the Ascots. The tone of the letter is respectful and complimentary of the house, but direct in stating that the many issues raised by the various inspections were new information to them about key systems of the house that are "health and safety" risks if left in their current condition. If they had known all these repairs would be necessary upfront, they would not have agreed to pay what they did. They are willing to move forward, but only if they receive the full amount of the requested credit.

After a couple more responses back and forth via their respective agents, the Ascots attempt to break through the impasse by adding that they will take care of the "gas leak" issue as well as the guest house issue. Leslie restates her belief that the Gas Company will take care of the leak for free if one is detected. As for the guest quarters, Mr. Ascot is confident this will prove a non-issue, because it was all done "quite properly" by their friend those many years ago. This offer does indeed entice the Buyers to relent from their original request and they settle for a price reduction of $80,000. From their original asking price of $1,750,000, the Ascots are now under contract with the Castillos at $1,545,000.

With the sale of their home back on track, the Ascots move forward with the inspection of the home they are purchasing, and they employ several of the same inspectors that the Castillos used. All those inspections find that their downsize home is in pretty good condition and they resolve that process with a credit of $2,700 from that Seller. Their offer was an all-cash purchase. They had been competing with several other Buyers and Leslie had instructed them not to make their purchase contingent upon the sale of their current home - and they had agreed.

Mrs. Ascot calls the Gas Company and schedules an appointment for them to investigate the suspected gas leak by the gas meter. To her surprise, they come promptly later that same day. After poking around for about half an hour, the technician informs her that he has located a small leak at the meter and he has taken care of it. Just as Mrs. Ascot breathes a sigh of relief, he informs her that the gas system has at least one other significant leak "downstream" of the gas meter and, for safety reasons, he has to turn off gas service to the property until it is repaired. Bewildered, Mrs. Ascot asks that he complete those repairs now as she needs the gas for cooking, heating, and hot water. The technician calmly explains that the Gas Company is only responsible for all of the lines leading to the gas meter; the gas lines beyond the meter and into her property belong to her, and are therefore her responsibility. "Call a plumber," he adds over his shoulder while walking to his truck.

She frantically calls her plumber and he agrees to come first thing the next morning. She is comforted by his quick response and thinks, "One night without heat and hot water won't be that bad." The plumber comes the next day and quickly determines that there is a large leak in a line that leads to the garage and guest quarters. Inconveniently, most of that line is under concrete. Once he isolates that line from the rest of the gas piping, he conducts a pressure test, only to find that there must be a smaller leak somewhere else as well. He spends much of the day disconnecting heaters, water heaters, and other gas appliances in hopes of finding the smaller leak without any luck. He will have to return tomorrow, and start by following each gas pipe. He reminds Mrs. Ascot how difficult this process can be as the crawl space under her 1923-built home is quite small and he cannot get to all of the gas piping in the crawl space. He also adds that it could be in a vertical pipe within the walls of the house.

The plumber returns the next day with a helper and spends the day painstakingly searching for and inspecting all of the gas piping he is able to find. By the end of the day he is really worked up, and starts telling Mrs. Ascot that he may have to abandon the old gas pipes and install new gas pipes throughout the property, which will be expensive, and will require subsequent wall patching and painting wherever he has to break through. At this point Mrs. Ascot has not had hot water for three days and her long-time plumber is frustrated and unable to provide any clear answers.

She calls a different plumber that her friend suggests, who arrives early the next morning. She again describes everything that the Gas Company and her first plumber told her, and then the second plumber starts digging. He digs up through the garden and within a few hours locates the spot of the large leak leading to the guest quarters. He spends much of the day repairing that line, but a pressure test of the system shows there is indeed a small leak somewhere under, in, or around the house. He returns the next day to continue the search for this small leak and Mrs. Ascot commits herself to a fourth night without heat and hot water. The stress of all this is causing her psoriasis to flare up with a painful rash on the back of her neck.

On the fifth day, the plumber finally finds the smaller leak in an elbow joint in the gas line on the north perimeter of the house near the AC condenser, in a line that must have been added years ago when the laundry area was re-located next to the kitchen. The plumber makes the repair, the Gas Company completes their own "pressure test" and restores gas service, and the Ascots can finally take hot showers again. The gas leak repair that their agent assured would be "a free service by the Gas Company" cost $4,700, in addition to whatever the first plumber would want for the days he spent in vain.

During all these days without hot water, Mr. Ascot is suffering in his own quagmire of a very frustrating permit process. He has lived in this city for decades and feels quite comfortable going to the City Building Department to get his guest quarters permit taken care of himself. He brings a copy of those original plans, along with a copy of the permit annotated as "Expired", which Leslie received from the Castillo's agent. After waiting for over an hour, he finally gets to talk with a person at the front desk of the Planning Department. He shows his old plans, talks about what a great reputation his contractor had in this town, and asks that whatever clerical error took place, the old permit be signed and corrected now.

The employee leans under the counter, pulls out a copy of a stapled document and hands it quickly to Mr. Ascot, saying "Here is a list of what we need to get your permit process started."

"No, you misunderstand," Mr. Ascot explains. "I do not

want to build a guest quarters, it already exists, and these are those plans from 1983."

"Mr. Ascot," the clerk recites in a sort of monotone chant, "the ordinances have changed significantly since 1983. You will have to have these guest quarters comply with the current ordinances or they must be removed. We will need new plans and engineering before we can give you any sort of approval to make the changes required to permit the guest quarters that you built without necessary permits in 1983." Mr. Ascot asks how long this will take. The city employee responds that, depending on the changes necessary to get approval, it could take anywhere between two and six months. Mr. Ascot stalks out.

Back in his car, Mr. Ascot calls Leslie and yells that he cannot believe that they agreed to get the guest quarters permitted. She empathizes and reiterates that it's ridiculous, and that she has never heard of such a thing. Two weeks later, with $7,000 spent on plans and engineering, Mr. Ascot now understands that he has agreed to a $50,000+ upgrade to the guest quarters in order to have it permitted. Most of that cost will be foundation work to the garage below, as well as alterations due to new boundary set back requirements. The sale of his longtime home has turned into a nightmare with $80,00 price reduction, $50,000+ in construction and no way to complete the permit work in time to meet the close of escrow deadlines for the sale and the purchase.

He calls a real estate attorney in town and begs him for help getting out of the deal. He emails the attorney the purchase contract, inspections, and all of the other documents associated with the sale of his current home, as well as the home he and his wife are attempting to purchase. When they meet, the attorney reviews the possible outcomes:

1. Cancel both transactions: The Buyer of their current home files a Lis Pendens and sues for performance with a high probability of winning, with the results being the same costs, plus legal expenses and the loss of the deposit on their desired purchase (another $27,000).
2. Sue his listing agent: The same likely outcome, plus the added legal expenses of that suit.
3. Attempt to re-negotiate the agreement about permitting of the guest house: If the Buyer will take on that responsibility, they can close the sale as scheduled, allowing them to close on their desired purchase as well.

Feeling trapped, Mr. and Mrs. Ascot decide to attempt the third option. They instruct Leslie to attempt to re-negotiate the permit issue. She calls back to report that she "had no luck" and complains that the other agent is rude to her. Mr. Ascot writes a letter to the Castillos, and directs Leslie to deliver it via the Buyer's agent. The Castillos respond with an empathetic letter clearly stating that they only wish to have completed what has already been agreed to. They also understand that the permit process could take a lot longer than either party expected. They write that they are willing to close escrow and take on the completion of that project if they are given $75,000 to do so. They understand that the bids total approximately $50,000, but they are worried about the unknown risk of the city adding more to the project once it has begun. A few more anxious letters go back and forth, but they eventually settle on the Ascots giving the Castillos $67,000. Exhausted, the Ascots are able to close escrow; they are two weeks late, but they do finally close the sale of their home, as well as the purchase of their downsize home.

For the Ascots, the sale of their long-time home has been one of the most stressful times in their lives. After reducing their asking price by $75,000, they sold for $147,000 less than they had originally agreed upon with the Castillos, spent $2,200 in legal fees, and almost $10,000 in architect/contractor/city fees. Mr. Ascot has always struggled with migraines, and had three terrible bouts during the sale of his home, in addition to the psoriatic flares suffered by Mrs. Ascot. After such a terrible experience, the Ascots are pained to see Leslie's **Just Sold!** flyer arrive in the mail, with a picture of their long-time home on it, advertising how she had "**Done It Again!**"

The sad tale of the Ascots sale may seem to be an exaggeration of unfortunate events unrealistically compressed into one transaction, and I would agree- partially. The actions of the Castillos and their Buyer's Agent were actually quite normal for a well-informed principal and agent in the market today. Even the number and type of inspections were quite predictable. It is not the challenges that arose during the Ascot's transaction that made it so nightmarish, but rather, the helpless and reactive position in which they consistently found themselves. Could the Ascots have been in any other position, given all of the very real issues with their home? Could their agent have made a significant difference in their experience during the transaction and even affected the results? *Absolutely!*

Disclosure

There is a predictive process to selling a home, with a definable *beginning, middle,* and *end.* The primary reason that the Ascots experienced such a stressful transaction during the sale of their home was not the physical condition of the property. Rather, it was because, unbeknownst to the Ascots, Leslie ignored best practices and jumped right to the middle of the process. By placing their home on the market without preparing either the Ascots or their home, their agent skipped vital beginning steps. The sale of a home must begin with the necessary diagnostic step that first defines the condition of the home, and then determines its market value from that now defined condition. Leslie allowed the Castillos to discover the condition of the property, leaving the Ascots vulnerable to the costly renegotiation of the sales price and terms. She did not utilize one of the most powerful tools that a Seller has when preparing for the sale of their home – the disclosures.

Disclosures could be broadly defined as all those forms and questionnaires that the law requires a Seller complete and provide to the Buyer in a residential real estate transaction. All too often, agents (and therefore their clients) view these important documents as time consuming, unimportant nuisances of the transaction. I have often witnessed listing agents waiting until their client's home is under contract with a Buyer before they ask their clients to complete those necessary disclosure forms, which is a wasted opportunity to have solved potential problems well before the home ever went on the market.

In California, Sellers have several mandatory disclosures to complete in a standard transaction. One of those is referred to as the Seller Property Questionnaire. On the second page of that four page list of questions, the Seller is asked if they are aware of any "Ongoing or recurring maintenance on the Property," with the parenthetical example, "for example, drain or sewer clean out…" The neighborhoods I commonly serve were built 60 to 80 years ago, which happens to be the life span of the typical sewer pipe connecting a house to the main sewer line owned by the City. If a Seller answers "Yes" to this question, and explains that once or twice a year they have their sewer pipe "snaked", then they most likely have tree roots that have invaded that pipe. This makes sense when you consider that these neighborhoods have an abundance of mature trees. The root systems of these trees invade the underground sewer lines because they are commonly made of three and four-foot sections of clay pipes. These pipes do not have to be cracked to be compromised because the hair-like ends of these root systems can penetrate the joints between these small sections of clay pipes. If these invading roots have not been dealt with, they will thrive within the sewer pipe and not only block but also cause serious damage to the line.

Most often, the Seller will state that this is just a typical maintenance issue and the Buyer should not be concerned about having to continue this type of maintenance, and I agree that the Buyer could have this reaction- but it is not likely in the context of a typical physical inspection contingency period.

Before their home even went on the market, the Ascots could have hired a reputable sewer company to complete an inspection of the sewer line. How, you might be wondering, would this be any different from what the Castillos found in their sewer inspection? The choices the Ascots would have been given by such a pre-inspection. For example, if some roots are found in the line, a Seller can then pay to have the line cleaned of those roots with a hydrojet, and then have a detailed video inspection completed of the entire line. Often, what such an inspection will show is that the roots have compromised only a small portion of the line, and that large sections of the line are still in working condition. Armed with this knowledge, the Seller can deal with smaller repairs or replacements of the line at a greatly reduced price, as compared to potentially replacing the entire line at the Buyer's insistence. By anticipating the concern of a future Buyer, the Seller can clearly quantify that concern, and provide the appropriate remedy. Instead of providing the Buyer a worrisome and vague disclosure about having to "snake" the sewer every couple of years, a Seller can provide a very clear and well documented solution at a cost that was significantly less than the unnecessary replacement of an entire line of clay pipes. Acting proactively with just this one issue would have saved the Ascots about $20,000.

Therefore, if the listing agent has the disclosures from the Seller before placing that home on the market, then they can identify issues that could potentially derail the future escrow and assist the Seller with more clearly defining those issues by answering three simple questions: What is the condition? What is the remedy? What is the cost of that remedy?

For the Ascots, the HVAC system inspection could have gone quite differently if the disclosures had been completed prior to marketing of the home. From the same Seller Property Questionnaire mentioned earlier, the listing agent could have been forewarned about the age of the heating and air units in the Ascot's home. Though a listing agent is not a contractor nor expected to be one, they should be familiar with the inspection process and the systems scrutinized in typical physical inspections. In this case it would be quite clear to a diligent agent that the Ascots had upgraded only half of the heating and air system, and those over 30 years ago. This is enough information for a listing agent to know that at best the heating and air systems are functional, but beyond their intended life expectancies. If a typical Buyer is left to discover this during the inspection period of a transaction, the listing agent can predict that the Buyer will want a credit for some or all of what a new heating and air system will cost. In other words, the agent can pre-identify a future negotiation.

What can be done? First, the Seller could have a reputable HVAC contractor inspect the HVAC system. In the Ascot's case, a contractor would have found the same issues that the Castillo's inspector found in the Hell Scenario: a very old heating and air system serving the first floor with an asbestos issue, and a "newer" system from the mid 80's serving the second floor. You may ask here, "So what's the difference? Won't the systems cost the same to replace?" The answer is timing. Prior to going on the market, a Seller is able to make an HVAC decision that will then pass muster during a future transaction. Prior to marketing, the Seller has greater control. They can ask their listing agent, "Do we need an entirely new HVAC system to pass our future inspection?" and their agent can provide that answer. In the Ascot's case, the old system on the ground floor which still has a gas powered AC unit with a pilot light is not going to pass inspection, and the asbestos material on the ducting of the downstairs unit is not going to be well received by any future Buyer. On the other hand, if the unit serving the second floor is functional and can be safely operated for a few more years, then there is a credible argument for not updating this system. The Ascots could have then decided to replace the downstairs HVAC system with the added benefit of having time to obtain competitive bids to do so. The positive results of just this one pre-inspection are many, empowering the Seller with the selection of the contractor, competitive bids, savings, and even possibly raising the sales price.

What about the roof? There are two disclosure forms in which the Seller answers a series of questions and has the additional opportunity to supply narratives to some of those questions. One is titled the Transfer Disclosure Statement. One of the specific questions a Seller has to answer on that disclosure is the type of roof the property has, and whether or not the Seller knows the approximate age of that roof. The Ascots could have answered this prior to marketing their home by stating that they have a Spanish Tile roof that is more than 40 years old. An agent in Southern California quickly learns that

Spanish roofs are beautiful, long lasting, expensive, and very brittle. Rather than wear out, the individual tiles suffer most of their damage when the homeowner or any contractors walk on the roof for any reason. That the Buyer's inspectors found hundreds of broken tiles on the Ascot's roof is not surprising. But what could have been done differently?

This should be an easy strategic decision for a good listing agent to suggest, since that agent knows that the Buyer will always have the roof surveyed during the inspection process. Leslie could have recommended inspecting it prior to selling the home. The cost to repair or replace hundreds of Spanish tiles as well as other general roofing "tune-ups" can be completed for only a couple of thousand dollars. That tune-up would typically involve replacing and repairing the broken tiles, re-securing any that are out of place, and cleaning off leaves and other debris that may have become trapped on the roof, behind the chimney, and in the rain gutters. After taking such preliminary steps, when the roof is later inspected by the Buyer's inspector, he or she would find an older Spanish tile roof in good working order. Even if that same inspector finds that the underlayment is at or near the end of its life, the discussion with the Buyer now centers on the importance of maintaining the Spanish tiles, rather than negotiating the cost of an entirely new roof. In the Ascot's case, this would have saved several thousand dollars while also eliminating a specific stress from a difficult transaction.

But what about an issue with a foundation? Surely that is not an issue that could be dealt with as easily as the roof? Perhaps, but the process is the same – inspect, describe, quantify. In the completed disclosures, a Seller will list the repairs and upgrades they have completed while living at the home. In the Ascot example, it is noted that their home is built in 1923. In the neighborhoods in which I primarily work, the building codes changed significantly in 1933, especially the foundation codes. If the Ascot's had not retrofitted or "bolted" their foundation, then a knowledgeable agent would know that a prospective Buyer would understandably have concerns about this issue. Again, to rely on my experience with the neighborhoods where I primarily work, if a foundation is not bolted, we can make two predictions about our future prospective Buyer:

1. Their general physical inspector will recommend that they have a separate foundation inspection.
2. The Buyer will have difficulty securing standard homeowners insurance.

As for the first issue, if it is known that the Buyer will request a separate foundation inspection, would it not be better for the Seller to be able to consider the information such an inspection will contain long before hand? In the Ascot example, the Castillo's inspector found that there were both significant cracks in the foundation and that the foundation was not bolted. The majority of the foundation credit given by the Ascots was for the replacement of several linear feet of foundation where the cracks were found. It is actually quite common for cracks to be found in a foundation and it is predictably alarming to the Buyer to hear of such cracks. The situation is ripe for a contractor to say that the only "safe" repair is the replacement of that portion of the foundation. This is where the value of a very good foundation expert is demonstrated. Just as every cracked tooth does not require extraction by a dentist, not every cracked foundation requires replacement. A good foundation expert can assess cracks based on size, location, and other relevant factors, then provide appropriate options such as epoxy filling, strapping, underpinning, a combination of these, and/or replacement. Given the advance opportunity, the Ascots could have opted to properly repair the cracks, pre-disclosed that information to prospective Buyers, and even pre-negotiated all or part of the expense of bolting with their selected Buyer.

I have observed that Buyers welcome thorough disclosures from a Seller and tend to think well of the Seller for doing so. On the other hand, Buyers left to discover serious conditions that are not pre-disclosed by the Seller, tend to believe the Seller purposely omitted this information and react punitively.

Though sewers, roofs, and foundations may not be the most relevant details of a transaction where you live, can we now agree on the need for you and your agent to identify those issues that are most relevant to the sale of your home prior to being in a transaction with a Buyer? Would you not feel much more empowered to have the opportunity to deal with those issues well ahead of the pressures of a transaction?

Not all pre-marketing inspections are for the purpose of fixing a physical problem. They can also help to re-define a physical characteristic of a property. Chimney inspections are a helpful example. Chimneys are relatively expensive structures that nobody expected to see the inside of once they were built, including the average homeowner. They are typically built to provide a function, rather than be judged on visual appeal. And yet today, these systems are being given detailed video inspections in a typical real estate transaction. This might sound odd, but a chimney is analogous to a sewer line in its intended function. Much like a sewer line can be quite rough on the interior of the line and still perform its function of moving waste water off the property and into the sewer system, an old masonry chimney is designed to allow the orderly escape of hot gases safely out of a home. The masonry of the inside surface was never meant to be judged beyond its performance of that transfer of heat while maintaining its structural integrity. Video inspections of the inside of a chimney tend to veer from that standard of performance into the realm of perceived visual imperfections. The result is that these video inspections tend to convince a Buyer that a chimney is unsafe to use unless a lot of money is spent to "repair" these perceived dangers, and often such conclusions are reached without any evidence of actual heat damage to any structure of the house. What I am trying to say, while not throwing all such inspectors under the bus, is that I see a great deal too much selling of unnecessary repairs during a lot of chimney inspections.

This being the case, the Ascots could have had their chimneys inspected before they ever went on the market. Since their home was built in 1923, it is not at all shocking that their chimneys were constructed without well-lined flues. A full disclosure of their condition to the Buyers prior to making an offer would have taken care of the issue right up front. Armed with those reports, the Ascots could then fully explore their options. For example, the listing agent could have suggested moving forward with the necessary rain caps, spark arrestors, and other minimal repairs, which would allow the fireplaces to be safely used for gas fires rather than wood burning fires, which burn much hotter. With that small amount of work completed, Leslie could have provided this information to the Castillos and redefined their expectations of the chimneys. They may have embraced the preserved character of those chimneys and accepted that the fireplaces could still be enjoyed, albeit exclusively with gas fires rather than wood burning fires. Again, we see the potential to eliminate a stressful issue while saving the Ascots several thousand dollars.

In comparison, electrical findings tend to be a bit stickier. Again, even without the Seller stating that they have updated the electrical system, the listing agent really should know at a minimum that any wiring from 1923 could have a negative impact on the transaction. Where I work, it is common that wiring in the 20's was what is known as "Knob and Tube" wiring. This type of wiring is not in conduit, but runs exposed between small insulated posts throughout a house. The danger with this type of wiring is threefold: the outlets to which it leads are typically not grounded, the wires themselves are not safe to the touch, and they can cause fires if they are in contact with the kinds of boxes of things people tend to store in their attics and basements (where such wires are typically found). An electrical issue such as this is different from the other issues we have explored. Even though the older chimneys were found unsuitable for wood burning, they could be presented as suitable for gas fireplaces without any real loss of value. No such functional change can be applied here. Electricity needs to be safely distributed in a house and that is difficult to do via knob and tube wiring. What options might a Seller have before placing their home on the market?

The greatest opportunity afforded to a Seller in a case such as this is the chance to select a good electrician to give a dependable bid to replace the old wiring. Realistically, this can only be completed with competitive bids. Now that the Seller knows the cost or has quantified this electrical issue, the Seller can decide if it is advantageous to complete this work beforehand, negotiate a credit with the Buyer during the general negotiation, or a combination of the two. In the Ascot's case, where they expect that their future Buyer will likely complete significant remodeling, then they have the opportunity to negotiate some percentage of that cost upfront, from zero cents on the dollar with multiple offers, to 50 or 75 cents on the dollar with just one Buyer. In this example, the Ascot's doing the electrical replacement and then repairing the plaster walls and ceilings after that replacement would be a waste, since they expect that the Buyers are going to be opening those walls again during their remodeling. In other words, the optimal solution can be considered beforehand as compared to making that same decision during escrow with all its pressures, timelines, and the Buyer's added demands.

So what about the Ascot's ill-fated decision to have the guest quarters permitted? Based on what he remembered from the original project, Mr. Ascot assumed that finalizing the permit would just be a clerical issue. Is it fair to blame this too on the listing agent? I believe so.

Permits are a bit of a hot potato in real estate. That permits are important is undeniable, but many real estate brokers do not want their agents getting involved with permits at all. Why? Liability. If an agent makes incorrect representations about the permit file of a given property, they may be financially liable for their incorrect representations. This may be area specific, but where I work, Buyers are keenly interested in the permit history of a property they are considering. Their fear is that if an addition to a home that they purchase is found to be without proper permits, then the local government body could force them to remove that addition. Plainly, they do not want to pay for a structure that they could be forced to remove at a later date.

So, in the case of the ill-fated Ascot sale, Leslie should have expected that most interested Buyers would specifically ask "Is the guest quarters permitted?" She did not need to become an expert in city planning or the permit process, nor does your future listing agent. They should, however, give a cursory review of the permit file of a given property and make note of anything that the eventual Buyer would during the inspection contingency period. In this case, the agent could have alerted the Sellers that "Expired" was stamped across the permit for the guest quarters. Again, this provides the Seller an opportunity to make the best decision possible prior to their home even going on the market. They could consider ahead of time what it would take, both in time and money, to correct the problem, or they could decide to include this knowledge and its explanation in their disclosures to all of the future interested parties. This would avoid the kind of fateful decision our Mr. Ascot made, which was essentially agreeing to sign a blank check on behalf of the Buyers. The listing agent has to be able to step in and make their client aware of the possible ramifications of all courses of action they are considering. When this subject comes up with other agents who work in similar neighborhoods, I am amazed when I hear comments like "My broker does not allow me to look at the permits." Can you imagine going to a doctor that refuses to look at the x-rays of your injured leg because it will increase their liability?

It is worth noting that even if Leslie had diligently followed through with the Sellers in identifying and pre-inspecting those issues that would be a concern to their eventual Buyer, the Ascots could not have avoided all of the issues that arose. The gas leak is a great example of an issue that could not be predicted or resolved well before placing the Ascot's home on the market. Sometimes there are issues that are discovered during the Buyer's inspection process that really are a surprise to all involved and are clearly the responsibility of the Seller to remedy. And because such issues can, and likely will, arise, it is all the more important to deal with as many predictable issues beforehand as possible.

I have seen some truly odd things discovered about a house during escrow, from a property built beyond its lot lines to a raccoon that just gave birth to a litter within the walls of a house. Clearly the Seller did not know, and just as clearly the Seller has got to remedy the condition, and fast. The gas leak example is a very real one- and it happened to me during the sale of my own home in the summer of 2015. Though I had completed all of the relevant inspections and disclosures prior to opening escrow with the Buyer, their inspector did detect "a gas smell" by the gas meter. I called the Gas Company and everything in the Ascot's gas adventure happened to me and my wife.

All in all, the Ascots could have saved well over $100,000 if they had just been advised of the benefits of pre-inspecting some noteworthy issues that become apparent during the completion of the mandatory disclosures. That savings is a direct result of simply being given the opportunity to make some good, proactive decisions prior to marketing their home rather than deferring those same decisions until they are under contract and stuck negotiating reactively with a Buyer. With the benefit of experience and the Seller's disclosures, the listing agent could have advised this course of action and provided the optimal time for the Sellers to consider these issues.

There is no credible reason to limit this optimization of the decision process on behalf of the Seller. The motivation of a good listing agent from disclosures to the end of the transaction is to create a space in which the Seller is provided the opportunity to make good decisions at the optimal time; from pricing, presentation, marketing, negotiating, and all the way through the closing.

Evaluation

We have reviewed together the very real dollars lost and the unnecessary anxiety suffered by the Ascots because their agent did not take advantage of the opportunities gained by completing the disclosures with them prior to marketing their home. We saw how those disclosures actually could have given the Ascots the optimum time to consider the physical condition of their property and make the best decisions about those issues. Now we are moving forward to evaluation and pricing the home, the next steps in the beginning phase of selling a home, with this idea of optimizing the decision process still in mind.

Like most Sellers, the Ascots believed the only important decision to make in marketing their home was what price to ask. As you might recall, when they first listed their home with their agent, they decided what to ask for their home based mostly on what their neighbor's home had sold for recently. Such a process of determining the listing price seemed fairly obvious, so they, like many people, did not think much more about it. If their agent had provided them a thorough evaluation of their home's real value in the market, they could have had the opportunity to price their property effectively for a higher dollar outcome.

In my day to day experience, the evaluation process begins with a potential client texting, emailing, or calling to ask "What is my home worth today?" They are often disappointed when they hear that I have a two-step process for providing that answer. "First," I explain, "let's meet together for a tour of your home. Once I have walked through it with you, I can return in a few days and review a written evaluation of your home with you." Their initial surprise and disappointment is not surprising to me. More and more frequently, potential clients who reach out have already sought an instantaneous online "Free Estimate" of the value of their home. They have also probably watched one of any number of celebrity real estate shows where the agent arrives at a grand estate, has a quick look around, and declares on the balcony "I can sell your home for $12,000,000!" So why should I need a tour and a few days' time to determine the value of their home? To be accurate. Online and computer generated evaluations most often provide an approximate value within 20% of a given property's true market value, which is frankly not an accurate enough estimation for the homeowner to make all of the necessary decisions to obtain the best results. Providing an accurate evaluation of a property can be quite challenging, but absolutely worth all of the time and effort it takes to do so well.

Providing the answer to "What is my home worth today?" is a surprisingly subtle exercise:

The evaluation of a property's current market value is a thought experiment, in which one attempts to correctly predict how a set of unknown Buyers are going to react to the availability of a given home, based upon how a similar but unknown subset of Buyers reacted to similar properties in a similar location in the recent past.

This experiment gives us the variables that we need to clearly define, which will then provide us the answer as to what the subject property is worth today. Those three variables are similar properties, similar locations, and the recent past.

Since we will be comparing in some manner the subject property to "similar properties", the very first step to take is to define what the subject property actually is. This seems so obvious as to be overlooked by the homeowner as they have lived within their home for years. As I have not lived in their home for years, and perhaps have never even been to it, a visit and tour is necessary. But even before seeing the property with the owner, there is some research for me to do. I find it extremely helpful to start by reviewing the public records of the subject property. The first of those is the tax assessor's records in which basics, such as the square footage of the dwelling and the lot, the year the house was built, and the number of bedrooms and baths, are listed. I then review the permit file for the subject property, which gives glimpses into the history of the home such as the original owner, builder, and architect. Also listed are many of the repairs, additions, and improvements that have been completed at the property and when.

This prior familiarity with the property greatly enhances that first tour of the property. By listening attentively to the owner and asking questions, I obtain richer details about the property beyond just the basics of size and number of bedrooms, such as the quality of the design, finishes, and maintenance. I can also note structures and improvements that may not be reflected in the written records.

Once I have reviewed the written records of the subject property and learned even more from the owner, I have a clear understanding of what the subject property actually is, and can begin the homework of evaluating the current market value of the subject property. I start with defining the parameters, or subsets, within which to consider the given property. Thankfully, an agent does not have to consider every house that has sold in a given city or county in order to evaluate the value of a given home within that area. Rather, the next step is to define what we mean by "similar location", which is defined as the neighborhood in which the subject property resides.

To all those that live within a given city, the boundaries of the neighborhoods within that city are well known. When city locals meet for the first time they will often say something along the lines of, "You live in Pasadena too? What part?" The "part" they are referring to is the name of the neighborhood-whether it is officially designated with that name or just known locally as such. That neighborhood could be defined by certain streets, a geographic marker such as those homes north of the river or on the south side of train tracks, or the boundaries of school districts within the same city.

Even an experienced appraiser that evaluates the value of homes for a living can be far off the mark in their conclusion if they are unaware of the boundaries of a given neighborhood. Often appraisers will default to considering properties within a one-mile radius of a given home, but could actually be looking at parts of three very different neighborhoods in doing so. This is just one of the reasons that local knowledge is so vital to this process.

Once we have determined the neighborhood in which the subject property resides- for example, we have defined it not just North West Glendale, but that part of North West Glendale that is west of Brand Boulevard, north of Kenneth Road, east of Grandview Avenue, and south of Cumberland Road- we can then move on to selecting the "similar properties" within that specific neighborhood to which we will compare the subject property.

Next, we have to define "similar properties", which seems a rather broad and open ended phrase. This is the trickiest variable of all, because even in the same neighborhood, individual homes can be vastly different from one another. In the North West Glendale area mentioned above, there are homes of various styles including Spanish, English, East Coast Traditional, Italianate, and even mid-century moderns. How can we possibly compare a Spanish Revival home built in the 1930's with a modern Post and Beam built in the early 60's? And architectural style is just one of the many differences between homes in a neighborhood. There is construction quality, floor plan, state of repair/dis-repair, upgrades, view, size of lot, landscaping, and a host of other very real attributes of a given home that are noticed, considered, and experienced by a typical Buyer in their consideration of a given property.

Do we need to come up with a long list of attributes that make up a home, assign enumerative values to each attribute, and then total that sum to determine what the property is worth? How would you go about assigning objective values to subjective attributes anyway? Some people love and highly value a pool, while others will consider the same pool a liability and a detraction from the property. Any summation of attributes will prove wholly unreliable due to the subjective value given to those many individual attributes. Fortunately, a much simpler bit of math provides a more objective context in which to effectively compare homes with so many differences.

When one looks at the sales of homes in a given neighborhood in the "recent past", which for our purposes we will define as the last 180 days, it is very useful to determine the average price per square foot (sf) that homes are selling for in that neighborhood in that time frame. The obvious and most common misuse of this tool is a homeowner that firmly believes that if their home has 2,000sf of livable square footage and the average dollar per square foot ($/psf) in their neighborhood is $500, then their home automatically has a market value of $1,000,000. This is a clear case of the danger of a little bit of knowledge. If one actually plots a graph of the $/psf that homes have sold for in a given neighborhood in a given price range, one will produce a shape very familiar to every student who has ever had a class graded on a curve- the upside down bell curve.

The important thing to note is the spread or occurrence of deviation that this bell curve would illustrate: most of the sales are within 10% above or below the average $/psf. It is also important to note that there are notable outliers of 20% or more. Therefore, in a given neighborhood the question to answer is "Where in the graph will a particular home be if it were to sell today?" In other words, simple math will give a very simple approximation of the value of a home in a given

he answer is that oldest adage of real estate,
n, location."

ods that are desired by more people are worth
more than neighborhoods that are not. For example, where I
live in Glendale, lots of people like to vacation in the summer
in Newport, California, especially in a neighborhood known
as Balboa Island. Glendale is a very nice neighborhood with
an average $/psf of about $500. On the bay front of Little
Balboa Island, homes will sell between $1,500 to $2,000psf.
Why? Because a square foot of land next to the harbor looking
out over the ocean is more desirable than a square foot of land
on my block in Glendale – simple, old fashioned supply and
demand. But why is this true? Well, if you built a 1,000sf beach
shack on a 4,000sf lot on Bayfront of Balboa Island it would
sell for around $6,000,000. That same shack built in my neigh-
borhood would sell for about $600,000. Both of those sales
greatly exceed the average $/psf of their respective neighbor-
hoods because the ground on which they are built has a market
value- and if the home on a given lot is small it does not degrade
the intrinsic value of the land on which it sits. That land value
is the underlying worth of a given location- and some are in a
nice location, while others like Bayfront or Park Avenue are
location, Location, LOCATION.

On the bell curve we do, as expected, see some outliers
that are 20% and even 25% above and below the average price
per square foot of a given neighborhood. Those that are well
below the average usually have significant attributes that are
considered negatives by a majority of the Buyer's pool, i.e. a
home located next to a gas station or a freeway on-ramp, or a
very small lot in comparison to what is common in that neigh-

borhood. On the positive side, a home well above the average could have a very large lot in comparison to the neighborhood and/or an exceptional view of the city.

Therefore, a home that has been tastefully updated on a large lot with a desirable view is a good candidate for being that outlier 25% above the average price per sf in that neighborhood – but it is not going to be 50% or 100%. **A home can elevate in value within the context of its neighborhood – but it cannot elevate itself beyond that context.** The pool of current Buyers is hyper aware of the marketplace for the short time they are in it, and generally, they prefer to "upgrade" the location in which they make their purchase before they overpay for an exceptional home within a less favorable neighborhood.

To illustrate: I often work in a neighborhood known as Sagebrush in La Cañada, CA. La Cañada is a highly sought-after neighborhood, because of the outstanding reputation of its public schools, so the land has a higher market value than its surrounding neighborhoods, like Glendale, La Crescenta, and Altadena. Sagebrush, however, is in a particular neighborhood within the City of La Cañada that is not within the La Cañada School District. This one factor proves so critical in this neighborhood that homes on one side of a street that go to La Cañada schools will sell for $250,000 to $400,000 more than the same size and style of home on the other side of the street that is not included in the La Cañada school district.

Homes that are more desirable to more Buyers in the market will be above the average $/psf for a given neighborhood. Conversely, those homes with attributes that are not desirable by most Buyers will sell well below that average $/psf because of its negative attributes. It is essential to know what attributes current Buyers will consider positive attributes and which they will consider as negative. Admittedly this does sound subjective and for good reason - it is! It is this subjective element that is dynamic and area specific- the factors that sway a subject property's market value may be very different in your part of the country. It is also this subjective element which prevents the current online "estimates of value" from being much more accurate than plus or minus 20%

The evaluation of homes with well-maintained character provides a helpful illustration of this variable. This type of home has the potential to sell above the average $/psf - but not always. If this home has a location that most Buyers will believe is a negative, like being on a high traffic street, then all of its positive features may be able to counteract that large negative and bring it back to the average $/psf for that neighborhood.

I work in a neighborhood rich with pre- and post- World War II homes. Many of the post WWII homes were built in the mid-century style, and were considered the least attractive of the character homes in this area in the 1990's. With a limited audience (or a smaller subset of the Buyer's pool), they tended not to sell for as much as the same sized Spanish Revival or Colonial in the same neighborhood. Today, this mid-century styled home is the most sought after style in the marketplace, and routinely sells for a 20 and 25% premium above the average $/psf. Fashion is dynamic and evolving, which makes the comparison process involved in the price of acquisition anything but static. In the 90's, I helped my friends Bob and Danielle purchase a 1955 Post and Beam in Glendale that was in original condition from the actual owner/builder. They purchased the home because they love that style – but at the time it was not considered a positive attribute in the marketplace and it did not sell for a premium. Today that home is worth a high premium in its neighborhood. Who is to say which style of home will be the most sought after in 20 years? Do you see how this subjective weighting of the positives and negatives determines where on the bell curve the home will sell?

The same oscillation in market value can be said of the interior decorating of a given home as well. Every year my wife, Andrea, and I love to attend the Pasadena Showcase Home. It is a great local tradition that has raised a tremendous amount of money for charity. Each year a committee selects a grand estate in the Pasadena area in which very talented designers and craftsman volunteer to show off individual areas or rooms of the estate with cutting edge design and remodeling. The result is a reinvigorated estate featuring the best in that featured design. A few years ago, I purchased a coffee table book commemorating 50 Years of Pasadena Showcase Design Houses. Though a beautiful book, I cannot think of a better example of how dynamic and changing interior design actually is. Each of the homes in the book is a snapshot of its design year. If any of those estates were brought to the market today, many of their interior designs would be considered a negative attribute and adversely affect the eventual sales price.

Floor plan is a less obvious variable, but still critical in the evaluation of the value of a home. We tend to think of good architecture as seen in the style of a home, but good architecture is also discerned in the quality of living it enhances or inhibits for those actually living within it. I have seen several 1,500sf homes with good floor plans that are more valuable than an 1,800sf home with an odd floor plan.

To this point, I often think of my own Norwegian immigrant parents. They purchased a two bedroom, one bath home of about 1,200sf in 1955. It was a square faux Spanish in a working class neighborhood. When they found themselves with four children in two bedrooms, they tried to divide one of the bedrooms into two so that their daughter was not in the same room with their three boys. But they soon felt they needed more room, so they added about 400sf to the back of the house. Rather than hiring an architect for such an endeavor, they tacked a 20 x 20 square room directly to the back of the house. My oldest brother moved into this new room, and my other brother, Kenneth, and I shared the original smaller bedroom, which had now become the connection between the original front of the house and the new square tacked on to the back of the house. It was not until 1989 when I was preparing to market this home for my parents that I realized my childhood "bedroom" was actually a hallway (with an alcove for bunk beds). That flawed floor plan was considered a strong negative by the market and my parent's home sold for well under the average for the neighborhood at that time. I regret being so inexperienced at that time and not being able to help my parent's home perform better in the marketplace.

I hope it is clear after these examples that location, size, style, floor plan, maintenance level, school district, lot size, and a host of other variables need to be considered and then compared to the average in a particular neighborhood of similar sized homes to predict what a Buyer will pay for a given home. Let's walk through the evaluation of an actual property together. It would be fun to use an extraordinary home as the example, but I fear it would not be as helpful to you. I think a more "ordinary" home for its neighborhood will actually serve as a more useful example.

In the spring of 2015, I was contacted by the owner of an 1,800sf home in my neighborhood. I reviewed the written records for that property and toured the property with its owners before beginning a Comparative Market Analysis of the home. This particular home is on a lovely residential street with larger, more expensive homes around it. It was built in 1955, and is a nice amalgam of pre-WWII traditional with a high pitched roof, but with a more mid-century design on the interior. The interior is very well maintained; both of the baths are in well preserved condition, and the kitchen has been tastefully updated. On the south quadrant of the rear patio, the owners had built a very cool outdoor family room with a covered roof and open walls on three sides, with a built-in sound system and a large flat-screen TV. This side of the street on which their property resides has upslope backyards rather than flat ones, but these owners have cleverly landscaped the yard by building a walking path meandering up the hill, with a small view deck near the top. Even though this property does not have a standard flat rear yard, by transforming their patio and upslope yard into its own destination, they have converted a negative attribute into a positive.

Since the average price per square foot in this neighborhood, locally known as the Verdugo Woodlands, was $435 per square foot at that time, I began by reviewing every sale in this neighborhood from the last 12 months between $700,000 and $900,000. While wading through these historical sales, it became clear that this home compared favorably to all of the homes that sold in the $700Ks. In the $800K range, this property compared favorably well into the mid-800's. Below a million dollars in this neighborhood, the market has quantum levels, or increments, of value of approximately $50,000 intervals. As I noted before, this home compares favorably to the homes that sold up to $800,000 in the last six months even though many of these homes were larger than the subject property. This was as I expected, and the subjective variables of this home all indicated that it would sell for a premium in this market. Now as I compare it to each of the homes that have sold over $800,000 I start to see homes that compare favorably to it starting at about $830,000 and certainly at those sales above $850,000. By favorably I mean homes that are likewise on good streets in this neighborhood, good character/design, are well maintained and upgraded, and have larger flat rear yards.

A helpful question to pose throughout the evaluation process is, "If this past sale were on the market at the same time as the subject home, which would a Buyer be more likely to choose?" At the point at which the answer is the other home rather than the subject property, I have reached the upper market value of the subject property. In this case the market value for the subject property is between $835,000 and $850,000. To be clear, we have now established what the recent sales indicated the "comparative market value" is for the subject property- but it does not necessarily mean that the property will sell at that price. All we have done is determine what the recent past is telling us about like-kind homes in this neighborhood; now we have to work on predicting what it will sell for in the near future.

First I need to review how the homes in this price range, $800,000 to $900,0000, are doing on the market now. I see that there are five homes currently in escrow in this price range and another eight available. Since I know that eighteen homes sold in this neighborhood in this price range in the last six months and that five are currently in escrow, I note the "absorption rate" of homes in this price range and neighborhood is about 3.8 homes a month, which indicates that there is just over a two month's supply of homes on the market in this price range in this neighborhood at present. Given that a neutral market that can neither be called a Seller's Market nor a Buyer's Market is about a six month's supply of homes, we are certainly in a Seller's market, one where there is a lack of inventory for the number of Buyers looking, in this price range in this neighborhood. Does this mean that the subject home will sell for more than its comparative market value? Perhaps, but not necessarily. Is the local market as a whole going up in value, down in value, or holding steady? The statistics for the local market in question show that it went up on average about 10% two years ago, and again last year and the first half of this year, but has been holding relatively steady since. Therefore, the context for this home in this neighborhood is a lack of supply in a market holding steady.

Now I compare the eight homes that are available on the market between $800,000 and $900,000 and note that most of these are a bit overpriced and are staying on the market for 30 days, 60 days, and some even more without selling. This may be due to agents or Sellers thinking there is a continued 10% increase in the market and that they can price their home 10% above their comparative market value- which is an incorrect use of valuable data. This also presents an opportunity for my client. That opportunity is the clear indication that there are more Buyers in the market than there are properties. These Buyers are not pursuing these other few homes on the market because they are priced too high. If I price my client's home correctly, I will attract multiple Buyers to my client's home and create a multiple offer situation for my client. The benefits of multiple offers to the Seller is not just obtaining a higher sales price, but the ability to select a Buyer that is better prepared to actually successfully complete the transaction at that higher price.

There are three kinds of Buyers in the marketplace: A, B and C Buyers.

The "C" Buyer is one that is motivated to purchase a home if they feel they can purchase it for under the market value-they are looking for a "steal."

A "B" Buyer believes that they are able and willing, but has not yet invested the time, or has not yet found an agent that will invest the time, to prepare them for the process of purchasing a home.

"A" Buyers are not only able and willing to purchase a home, but their agent has helped to actively arm them with the tools necessary to purchase a home. Their agent has verified that the Buyer actually has the down payment they will need, and can provide written proof of the same. The "A" Buyer is also pre-approved for the financing they intend to secure for the purchase of their home (Here I say "pre-approved" rather than "pre-qualified", but both terms have become a bit watered down in the marketplace). The "A" Buyer has selected a lender, a specific loan product, and completed a loan application with that lender for that specific loan product. The Lender, in turn, has checked that Buyer's credit, and verified the information provided on the loan application by reviewing such documents as that Buyer's last two years of tax returns, pay stubs, employment history, and source of funds. If this supporting financial data is not verified by the Lender, then the "pre-approval" is meaningless. In other words, the Lender needs to vet the Buyer to the extent that the underwriter will prior to issuing loan documents.

Buyers can only be deemed "pre-approved" when all of the specific verifications that will be demanded by the eventual underwriter have been provided by that prospective Buyer to their chosen Lender. So, an "A" Buyer has their down payment in liquid form and can provide proof of the same. This Buyer is also pre-approved for their proposed financing. These are both financial, objective, and measurable conditions.

Fully understanding their financial abilities as stated above, an "A" Buyer has made the decision to purchase a home within their financial abilities. Comparing their financial capabilities with their dream home, they have developed and accepted the limits of what they are able to purchase in their price range. This process involves deciding which variables they are willing to compromise and which they are not. They have decided that they have to have at least three bedrooms, but are willing to accept a smaller yard; or, they have decided on a specific school district and know they will get a smaller home than they had hoped in exchange for that district. They have decided that a view of downtown is paramount in their search for a home and they are willing to purchase a home that will need extensive renovation if they can get the view they want. They can clearly answer the question: "In this price range, what are you looking for?"

Lastly, the "A" Buyer understands the real estate market in the area in which they hope to purchase. They can walk a property with their agent and understand where in relation to the market value of that property the Listing Agent has priced it: at its value, overpriced, or underpriced. They have taken the time to walk through homes that have been on the market as well as reviewed the inventory of homes that have recently sold in their desired neighborhood. Their agent has educated them to the point where they are prepared to make a decision to pursue a home or not when it comes on the market. Their agent's role is not convincing them to purchase a specific home, but rather assisting them to be ready to make a good decision to pursue or not to pursue when a home in their price range, in their desired neighborhood, within their established parameters comes on the market. Why? Time. Desirable homes do not tend to be available for very long. At present where I live and work, a Buyer needs to make a decision to pursue or not pursue within the first five days a home is available, sometimes less. In other words, when a good home comes on the market, the Buyer does not have the luxury of unlimited time in which to consider the home. That is why it is critical for a Buyer to get their ducks in a row- down payment, financing, and wrestling with their search parameters- so that when a candidate home comes along, that Buyer can spend their time on the decision at hand, and are in a position to make the best decision possible.

Now that we know how important the distinctions are between the three types of Buyers, it is quite clear that a Seller should be targeting that subset known as "A" Buyers. Returning to our example Seller who has the benefit of the scarcity of like kind properties in their price range, they now need to consider what asking price will yield the highest results. As stated before, the recent sales indicate a market value of between $830,000 and $850,000. The current homes on the market appear to be priced a little high, which presents an opportunity for this Seller to attract those "A" Buyers that are currently in the marketplace. Some of these "A" Buyers have missed out on some past sales, as they were not chosen by previous Sellers in multiple offer situations. They are now even more ready to compete for the home they want and are even willing to pay a premium to stop being an "A" Buyer and actually secure a home- they are ready, willing, and able.

This Seller has the opportunity to sell their home for more than the recent sales seem to indicate. Common sense would state that they should then choose a price over $850,000 and see how high those "A" Buyers are willing to go. There have been years and markets where I would agree with that logic, but one has to accept that pricing is a marketing tool, and be aware of what tools are working well in the marketplace at a given time. When I started in real estate in 1988, the logic of pricing matched what you would think of as common sense- the asking price for a home was 5 to 10% above what the recent sales seem to indicate the home as worth. This left "room to negotiate." Nowadays, the market has grown accustomed to competing for a home by offering asking and well above the asking price if there are multiple offers. What is a bit counterintuitive is the clear observation that Buyers are acting more comfortable in pursuing a home if they know it already has offers, than if it does not. Though this may appear as counterintuitive, a Seller is wise to factor this observable truth into their pricing strategy. Other pricing strategies may be at work in your local market at any given time; it is vital to know what they are and which to employ to your greatest advantage.

Today, if a Seller in my local market prices their home 10% above its comparative market value, they run the risk of staying on the market for an extended period of time. To this they may say, "We are not in a hurry to sell our home! If it takes 3 or 4 months to sell for more, we are willing to wait." Again, that seems to be a good, common sense statement- but that does not make it true. Why? Because Buyers are extremely aware of how long a particular home has been on the market. Currently, if a home has been on the market for 15 days and has not received an offer, any Buyers considering that home will believe there is a significant reason why this is so- leading to the conclusion that it is overpriced. Though I am sure there is a good psychological/sociological reason for this behavior in the marketplace, I do not pretend here to understand it- I just observe it to be true in the marketplace today.

We clearly see the undeniable importance of time in this process- for both the Buyer and the Seller. While the Buyer is preparing themselves to be ready to make a good decision when a good candidate presents itself in the market, the Seller needs to prepare their property so that they can attract the best Buyers in their marketplace when they do present their home to that market.The Seller has a short lived opportunity to attract and negotiate with one or more of the Buyers in the "A" Buyers pool to yield a higher and better sale of their home. Because of how motivated the "A" Buyers are, they visit and consider a new home on the market very quickly. If that pool of "A" Buyers decides to not pursue that particular home, then the

Seller is left to deal with attracting the "B" and "C" Buyers at a lower price and less favorable terms.

For my example clients, this means pricing their home between $839,000 and $859,000 to attract more than one offer from more than one "A" Buyer, and seeing how high this competitive negotiation will go; $855,000, $865,000, or higher. After being diligent in preparing their home for market as well as intelligently pricing their home, the Sellers were rewarded with multiple offers and closed escrow for $885,000, which was at a $/psf of about 13% above the average at that time.

Presentation

Imagine for a moment that you were going to sell your car. You would likely want to clean it up before showing it to potential customers. You might take it to the car wash, vacuum up the little bits of gold fish crackers your toddler has spread over the back seats, and spritz the interior with a little Febreeze. It is just common sense- and yet, this kind of basic maintenance is shockingly uncommon when it comes to people selling their homes.

Most people take it as a given that a property would be presented to the market in its best light, but I cannot tell you how often I walk through a home that has been placed on the market and it looks like the Owners have not done a thing to prepare for Buyers and Agents to see it. Not just dishes in the sink, but rooms a mess with beds unmade, clothing all over, and even pet shit on the floor. I am not exaggerating. I have walked through an open house that was not only a mess, but had people sleeping in the bedrooms. It was so uncomfortable that I just wanted to get out of there as quickly as possible. Any such discomfort experienced adversely affects the perception of the very people the Sellers are hoping to attract to their property, causing it to sell for tens of thousands of dollars less than if they had simply cleaned up a bit. In this chapter, we will walk through the steps and identify the importance of a property's presentation.

There is a clear correlation between how a property looks and the price someone is willing to pay for it. I have observed that difference ranging from about a 3% difference on the eventual sales price to well over 10% - significant amounts of money in most real estate markets. Do you think our ill-fated friends, the Ascots, would have been willing to have a conversation about property presentation with their agent that could potentially net them between $45,000 and $150,000?

Like evaluation, presentation begins with a diagnostic step. First, I have to ask my client's permission to talk about their treasured home as it will be seen in the marketplace- as a commodity. And as a commodity, it will be viewed with a very critical eye. It is therefore crucial for the Seller to understand what the market will see when that critical eye is brought to bear on their property. To do so, a Seller needs to attempt to experience their own home as a Buyer would, to discern both the positive and negative attributes of the property. Once those qualities are clearly articulated, then presentation is simply a matter of highlighting the home's positive attributes and mitigating those that are negative.

A helpful way to discuss this is to remember that all properties have positive and negative attributes. My previous home, for instance, was an older English Tudor in a nice neighborhood. It had preserved original character and had been tastefully updated. Despite the authenticity of its Tudor elements, this particular style of home is not the most sought after in the current market. And though that neighborhood is in great demand, that house is sited on a corner lot with its back side just 10 feet from the road behind it, making the rear yard feel more like a side yard. Though the foundation had been retrofitted, past settlement of this home had manifest in the upstairs hallway not being quite level. All this to say, my house had some negative attributes that were going to limit how much it would sell for when it was placed on the market.

Since we could not alter how the house was sited on the property, we completed extensive landscaping to minimize that weakness of the lot, including planting tall shrubs that blocked the view of the close street on the back side of the house, and re-orienting the front walkway on the bottom third of the lot to create a very private, enclosed courtyard in what was the previously the side yard walk-way to the front door. These landscaping changes, which are relatively inexpensive, were effective in minimizing the effect of the odd siting.

The original interior floor plan was also a negative attribute of our home, as it was a compartmentalized 1920's floor plan. We calculated that significant dollars spent on the interior in updates would create a more open and modern floor plan and increase the market value of our home. On the ground floor, we opened the kitchen to the adjoining three smaller rooms, creating a modern kitchen that opens to one large great room. Upstairs, we combined two of the four bedrooms and one of the baths into a large master suite with an oversized master bath. When we sold that home in the summer of 2015, we had increased the market value of our home by 2.5 times the cost of all of those upgrades.

In that case, we confidently moved forward in spending well over $100,000 to prepare our home to sell. We had the time and determination to complete an extensive game plan before placing our home on the market. In most cases, though, the Sellers have already decided to sell and time, as well as good sense, may only justify minimal expenditures to show off a given property in its best light.

For example, I recently worked with a client selling a property on a street called "Olmsted"- for ease, I'll refer to the property as Olmsted from here on. Olmsted is a one story 2,500sf home in North West Glendale that had been lived in for over 40 years by one family. It was designed by an architect of local note in 1962. Its mid-century character is the most sought after style today, and most of that original style had been left in-tact by the Sellers, though they were open to completing some upgrades if they were warranted.

After reviewing the market evaluation together, we determined it was unwise to invest in significant upgrades. To be clear, I enjoy conceiving and completing upgrades to a property if it makes sense to do so. But in this case, we perceived that the location did not warrant a significant capital investment in this home. We decided to instead focus our efforts on highlighting the home's most marketable positive characteristics. First, we cleared the house of clutter, to emphasize the clean lines and elegant minimalism essential to its mid-century blood line. We then had the interior professionally cleaned, while our gardener cut and pruned the landscaping to show off the exterior grounds at their best. Lastly, we hired a stager to show off the great original character of key rooms with cool mid-century decor. Our goal was to attract a Buyer that loved this mid-century style who was willing to complete their own upgrades after they closed escrow.

By limiting the Seller's spending to less than $5,000 in market preparation, I felt we could market the home at $899,000 with multiple offers pushing the purchase price to as high as $950,000. If the Sellers were to complete significant upgrades such as painting, flooring, and remodeling the kitchen and baths, we would have had to market the completed project at well over $1,000,000, and I did not think this particular location was as competitive over $1,000,000. In this case, the Owner's net would be greater selling the property in its present condition with minimal expenditure, rather than the net they would have received if they invested $50,000 to $100,000 in that home prior to selling it.

This is an example of the quantum levels that exist in residential real estate. I like to compare it to the input of energy of heating water, which you may remember being demonstrated in your 9th grade science class if you had the amazing Mr. Pack as your teacher. He showed that it takes the same amount of energy to raise a cup of water from 35 degrees C to 36 degrees C as it does from 88 degrees C to 89 degrees C, but something very different happens once you reach boiling point at 100 degrees C. Suddenly, it takes a lot more energy to change that cup of water from 99 degrees C to steam at 100 degrees C. The water is not just heating up a one degree like before; it is a going through a phase change, from water in liquid form to water in gas form, which requires a lot more energy. Homes have an analogous point at which it requires a lot more energy (a different form of energy called "money") to go from one price range to the next. Every home reaches a point at which it becomes very difficult to add any more net value to it.

Perhaps another example might help- one that does not require you to remember anything from 9th grade science. I once assisted a client with a home in which he had invested over $200,000 in updates prior to placing it on the market. Like Olmsted, he purchased this home from a family that had lived in it for several decades. It is on a large, flat corner lot with the house sited just about in the middle of the parcel. Because the structure sits in the middle portion of the lot, it does not have a traditional rear yard like most properties in this neighborhood. Similar to my own home, which I referenced earlier, it has a good size side lot that was exposed to the street and did not feel private. The house itself was in very poor condition and in need of significant repair. Even more troubling was the floor plan. Though the house is about 2,500sf, the location of the rooms was odd. Off the entry was a huge living room that one had to walk through to get to the family room and the bedrooms. The three bedrooms were at three different corners of the rectangular house, with the children's room on the opposite side of the house as the master. Even if my client had updated each room and all of the systems of the house, he would have been left with a very unmarketable floor plan on an exposed lot with no obvious private yard space.

After spending considerable time at the property, we conceived of a change to the floor plan that would be quite marketable, as well as an extensive landscaping plan that would provide not one, but two private rear yard spaces, all the while preserving and enhancing the original Spanish revival character of the property. I hope while reading this you are cognisant of the risk this particular owner was taking. But the difference between this property and Olmsted is its location. This property is securely tucked into a sought after neighborhood of significantly more expensive homes. In other words, the finished product will not be overbuilt for its location, and will be similar to other homes in the immediate neighborhood that have sold in the hoped-for target price range above $1,250,000. This proved to be a case where the best decision was to invest the capital and time to realize the greater market value of this particular property. My client completed that project and we sold it for the targeted price.

I have had the privilege of working with this same client on over two dozen homes. I am selling one such property on the market right now as I write this for $2,395,000, and we have another coming on the market in a couple of months for around $1,300,000. On some we have done very little work before selling, while on others we have completed extensive work prior to marketing- but the decision process is always the same as we seek to answer that important question, "What is the optimal condition in which to present this property for the greatest return on the original investment?" This particular client actually owns a construction company, and has the liquidity to execute the changes and updates that we have determined will yield the greatest return. Even though most of us (average homeowners) may not have such capabilities, it is always best for the listing agent to offer the homeowner an analysis of the various options that homeowner has to elevate the value of their property before presenting it to the market place. If the money and time are not there to complete extensive upgrades, we still have many cost efficient and effective strategies proven to show off a given property at its best.

I have found that for most properties, wisdom sides with doing less rather than more. Always start with the basics, like the color scheme of the house, for instance. People often paint their home a color that they like, which is a personal choice. But once they decide to sell that house, the paint choices are no longer personal. They are a marketing decision. Does this "blue is my favorite color" Spanish home need to be re-painted a more traditional earth-toned color scheme to show off its character? The likely answer is yes. Consider such helpful questions as: How does the property look from the street? Is the landscaping covering too much of the house, or perhaps not enough? If the house has a view, do we need to trim trees to enhance that view? If the property is on a busy street or faces an unsightly property, can we plant a hedge or build a fence? Can the character be enhanced with new shutters or other such detail enhancement? What is appealing about the exterior of this house and what can we do to highlight or enhance that appealing feature? All of these examples can make a significant impact in the positive presentation of a home to potential Buyers without having to cost a lot of time or money to implement.

Once I have walked the exterior grounds with my clients and we have made note of changes that need to occur outside, we then walk the inside of the house. In each room I seek to answer "How can this room be best presented?" Often, there is simply too much Stuff. Instead of asking what to eliminate, decide what is essential to stay and get rid of the rest. Packing and moving personal items out of a room is relatively cheap in comparison to the financial return. Place what remains in a manner that works best to show off each room. I do not mean what makes the room work better for the homeowner, but what will make the space more appealing and therefore more valuable to the Buyers. Often these interior changes will feel uncomfortable for the Owner. Living in a house is very different from living in a house that is for sale. The latter is akin to putting on a play for a specific subset of the public known as potential Buyers. If the name of that play is Selling My Home for as Much as Possible, then some discomfort with living on a stage for a short time is worth the audience's approval.

Once the decisions are made about the personal items within the house, we can then move through the home with a critical eye that judges the physical aspects of the home in a binary way. Is the paint good or bad? Is the flooring good or bad? Is the tile good or bad? Each attribute of the interior is judged in this fashion with this clear context – will the cost of a change be worth the investment of time, hassle, and money to affect that change?

I like my clients to start by walking in the front door, and imaging they are seeing their home for the very first time. If the property has a formal entry, there should be very little in this space, other than a piece of art and a small piece of entry furniture. If we enter directly into the living room, then create a small open space in that room that feels like an entry.

It is best to display the formal living room as such, not a living room/family room/video game room/library/home office; there should be a sofa, coffee table, end table, comfortable chair, and some tasteful art. There should definitely not be a TV.

The dining area should be presented as a formal dining room: a table (not at its largest with all the leaves) set for entertaining, a light fixture centered over the table, and dining room chairs. The kitchen should be at its cleanest and lightest with almost nothing on the counters, nothing stored on top of the refrigerator, and definitely nothing displayed on the refrigerator with magnets.

The presentation of a bathroom should likewise be at its cleanest and brightest, with almost nothing on the counters, no magazine racks by the toilet, no toilet toupees, no furry rugs on the floor, and no kids toys in the bath or shower. Buyers have no interest in seeing anything that you actually use in the bathroom, like your tooth brush, hair dryer, shampoo, or skin care products. The shower or bath should only display one bottle of shampoo, that large bar of designer soap you never use, and an unused towel or two.

Bedrooms are best shown off in a simple, uncluttered manner. The kid's room needs only a bed, chest of drawers, homework desk, and perhaps some art (posters do not qualify unless framed). This is not the time for the occupants of these rooms to show off their individuality with walls painted their five favorite colors, or decorated with their favorite band posters or the poster of that girl from the Carl's Jr. commercial. The guest room should feature a bed, night stand, chest of drawers, interesting but limited art. Similarly, the Master bedroom should have a bed with a head board, night stands, chest of drawers, and art. If the room is large enough, including a cozy chair or sitting area is great. There should be no hampers, golf clubs, home office desk, or TV, unless it is flat and mounted on the wall. Remember, this play is showing off your home as having more than enough space for its inhabitants; they do not have to use the master bedroom as a home office.

The den or family room should feature a sofa and comfortable chairs, a coffee table, and some. In this room, it is appropriate to have a TV.

The home office should be clean, clean, clean, and as uncluttered as it would be if your boss was stopping by. If you are the boss, then it should be as clean as it would be if your mother were stopping by.

An important and often neglected area that benefits from the efforts of presentation are your closets. There should be nothing on the floor, and nothing on any overhead shelving. Hanging poles should be at no more than 60% to 80% of their capacity.

If your furniture and artwork do not show off the interior of your home at its best, get a bid from a professional stager for a room or even rooms. Good staging calls attention to the positive attributes of your home, not the pieces themselves. All too often, professional staging is confused with filling a space with rented furniture and knick-knacks. The eventual Buyers that you are hoping will be interested in your home can sense the poor attempt of manipulation that is the result of poor staging. Good staging helps them appreciate the space, and usually less is more in doing so. Sometimes I will have a stager simply arrange my client's existing furniture and sprinkle some touches of art and color around the interior.

At this point, we have gone through the interior of the property and have decided what stays, what goes, and what upgrades or repairs we are going to complete prior to marketing. All those that received a "yes" are scheduled, working backwards from the date on which the Owner wants their home to go on the market.

Do you think the Ascots would have benefited from such a discussion prior to marketing their home? With the help of their agent, they could have then decided what work, if any, they were willing to do to improve the marketability of their home before putting it on the market. Coupled with a thorough evaluation of their home, the Ascots could have considered proactively how to best price and present their home to the market in a manner that would have yielded the best results.

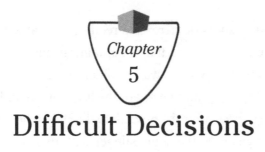

Difficult Decisions

Anyone who has been in the pressure cooker of trying to deal with an unfamiliar issue in a very high anxiety situation knows that the Ascots would have welcomed the opportunity to consider all of the relevant information prior to deciding upon the asking price of their home. I have a searing memory of being in such a high-stress situation myself. On July 3, 2015 my wife and I were completing a move after the sale of our own home. She was experiencing some discomfort, but we didn't think too much of it- she'd been moving so many boxes upstairs into our new place that it made sense for her hip to be a bit sore. But that soreness quickly progressed to an excruciating drive to the emergency room. She was admitted immediately and placed on a morphine drip for the intense pain running through her hip, down her right leg, and to the tip of her right foot. This pain trail, the subsequent x-rays, and a MRI convinced the orthopedic surgeon assigned to her case that a nerve in her lower back was impinged. The remedy seemed clear- epidural shots of steroids directly to the affected area in her lower back to reduce the inflammation that was applying pressure on that nerve. He was confident that she would experience relief quickly and be out of the hospital soon. His confidence was so great after the procedure that when he was talking with me, he gestured like a gunslinger with two six shooters in his hands firing rounds, Yosemite Sam style.

But the pain Andrea was suffering only increased. The obvious next step, as laid out by the surgeon, was simply to repeat the epidural procedure again; if that did not work, he would recommend surgery. "Sometimes," he now explained, "the epidural takes a second or even third time to provide the desired relief." This was new information to us. We approved the epidural procedure again, but this time the surgeon did not bother to speak with me when he was finished. What followed were several days of Andrea's continued suffering during a series of seemingly endless tests and procedures with different specialists. Though we trusted that the medical professionals were doing their best, they all seemed a bit too busy to explain it to us in terms we could understand.

On the morning of Andrea's eighth day in the hospital, the orthopedic surgeon announced that she would be released later that day. This made no sense. She was still in so much pain, with no clear diagnosis of what was causing it. Frankly, I was terrified. When the hospitalist assigned to us stopped in on her rounds, I blurted: "You are asking us to make decisions and we just do not have all the information we need. No one has really even explained the information we've been given. How can we make any decisions?" Her demeanor changed immediately. Finally, someone understood that we *did not* understand,

and she invested the time to explain all that was happening in Andrea's case. She also explained the realities of the pressure from the medical insurer to limit the expense of the treatment. We got it- there is a system of finite time and resources in which these medical professionals can treat a particular patient with all of the known and unknown variables of the diagnosis of that patient. We needed to make wise decisions within these limitations to best serve Andrea's illness. Since the diagnosis remained a bit nebulous, the best course of action was not to commit to another procedure or surgery, but rather, to move forward with physical therapy and pain management to the point of being able to return home and continue healing.

For the first month she used a walker. For the second and third she used a cane. Finally, she spent two months walking gingerly on her own. The reality was that Andrea injured herself during our move, which led to a cascade of issues that were not clear other than being excruciating. It resolved, sort of, with the lingering effects of a pinched nerve in her lower back and the slow recovery of that condition.

We learned through this experience that though we are not medically trained, there are times when we have to make medical decisions. Throughout her hospital stay, I had fantasized about a safe room in the hospital where each doctor that was working on Andrea's case would share all of their thoughts with us in simple language that we could firmly grasp. In this fantasy, the orthopedic surgeon would share all of his thoughts with us about Andrea's case and provide some context as to how her case compared to others he had dealt with in the past. The same would happen with the radiologist, then the internist, as well as the hospitalist. We could ask questions and get clarifications until we clearly understood the prognosis (or competing prognoses with their varying degrees of uncertainty) without having to attempt to discern through the heavy filter of the palpable fear of liability that so stunts meaningful communication in a hospital. We just wanted to understand all of the relevant information needed to make a good decision about how to best proceed with Andrea's care.

I wanted to be like Gene Kranz, the Flight Director that Ed Harris depicted in the movie *Apollo 13*. Do you remember that true story of Jim Lovell and his crew's ill-fated trip to the moon? On the way to the moon there is an explosion and the vessel is crippled. Not only is the original mission unattainable, but it is improbable that the astronauts can even return back to earth safely. Gene Kranz is in charge at mission control. In that room every system of the mission is represented by an expert: guidance control, medical, propulsion. Before launch each and every one has to confirm that their system is "Go for launch" and only after all report that they are ready does Gene allow the launch to proceed.

During that mission, Mr. Kranz demands and receives any and all information he requests from any of the systems experts. When the accident occurs, he calms everyone down and refocuses his team with the great line "Let's work the problem people! Failure is not an option." That's what I wanted, and needed, in the hospital with my wife in so much pain and her diagnosis still so undefined. I wanted to hear from each expert a clear presentation of their findings thus far so I could formulate a clear picture of what was happening to Andrea, what variables were known, and what variables were unknown, then we could weigh the risks of the possible next steps and move forward wisely in this medical crisis: "Let's work the problem people! Radiology? Orthopedics? Pathology?" Yet, instead of feeling like we were in charge of mission control, my wife was more like Major Tom "floating in a tin can, far,far away" and there was nothing that I could do.

It would be unfair to compare my wife's doctors to the Ascot's rather distant agent, but the stress and bewilderment my wife and I felt while in the hospital is similar to the reactive pressure cooker the Ascots found themselves in while selling their home. The important difference, however, is that my wife was in an unexpected medical crisis, while the Ascots were in a very predictable crisis that absolutely could have been avoided if their agent had created the space and opportunity for them to consider all of the relevant information that would have allowed them to make the best decisions possible.

This is the third level, the third dimension that the fiduciary responsibility allows an agent to perform if they are willing to do so. Whereas the responsibility of a fiduciary is most often perceived as a line that is not to be crossed, it can actually be an invitation to do so much more. Rather than a just a two dimensional boundary, it is a three dimensional space, that precious space where our clients make very important decisions, and it is the real sacred ground. And what is this added third dimension? That most precious of commodities, Time. It takes the expenditure of time by the agent to enter this sacred space.

And here we see the rub. The pay structure of the real estate agent is potentially misaligned for their client because of time. The Ascots had hired their agent to sell their home initially for $1,750,000 with a 5% commission of the eventual sales price, to be paid only when the sale of that property is concluded. Of that total commission, the listing agent (AKA the agent representing just the Seller and not the Buyer) will typically receive half, or 2.5% in this case. If the listing agent does sell the Ascot's home for $1,750,000 her total commission earned will be $43,750 (to keep things simple, I am not getting into the agent's "split" arrangement with her broker). The agent does not get paid anything unless the property sells. In other words, the listing agent agrees to assume the risk of time, effort, and marketing dollars for the agreed upon commission. In the Ascot's case, the sales price ended up being $1,493,000, so their listing agent's 2.5% commission was $37,325. Since the listing agent's commission is a set percentage, the pay structure seems perfectly aligned- if the house sells for more, then the agent's earned commission increases in the same ratio. Conversely, if the sales price decreases, then the agent's earned commission decreases accordingly.

Where, then, is the potential misalignment? Time. Remember that the listing agent is not guaranteed any pay when they take a listing. That being the case, how much time does one wish to commit to that listing? The Ascot's listing agent decided to invest very little time in preparing the property or the Ascots for the process of selling their home. She placed it on the market and reacted to whatever issues arose from then on until closing. While the Ascot's home sold for $207,000 less than they had asked, their agent's commission was only $6,425 less than if it had sold for full price.

Since it takes time to complete all that I have been describing in preparing to market a home, it is time that the listing agent is investing at their own risk. Can you recognize the potential for an agent to choose doing less, but doing less more often? To be blunt, perhaps the Ascot's listing agent moved quickly and similarly listed two other homes in the Ascot's neighborhood and made $37,325 each time for a total of $111,950. Can we now agree that there exists the potential for an agent to be more motivated by the volume of their sales rather than the quality of their performance within those sales?

Clearly, there is the very real potential for misalignment within the standard client/agent commission agreement. I see it in three different types of agents in the real estate marketplace: the one-dimensional real estate sale expeditor, the two-dimensional real estate salesperson, and the three-dimensional real estate professional.

The real estate expeditor is the agent that completes a transaction because they happen to be there. This is the agent who is chosen by the Seller as the listing agent because they are a favorite aunt's nephew that has a real estate license. This agent may have another "real" job and will help a friend by filling out the offer and submitting it to the listing agent. They may complete a handful of transactions in a given year, mostly as a Buyer's agent. They are akin to a waiter at a diner style restaurant- tell me which meal you would like from this menu and I will go in the kitchen and get it for you. They are not much of a resource for their client beyond access to the necessary forms and their familiarity with the offer and escrow process. They are there primarily at the point of sale, but not much more than that one dimension of the process.

The real estate sales person makes their living as a full-time agent. They can demonstrate their experience and compete with other agents successfully for clients, both Sellers and Buyers. They may take pride in their work and financial success, and they adhere to the common codes of conduct in the real estate industry. They steer their clients to the best of their ability towards the goal of a successfully closed transaction. They can be wildly successful and the "Number 1" agent in their company. But have you ever noticed how many "Number 1" agents there are in the market? The Ascot's agent is an example of this transactionally oriented agent. She did not cross the fiduciary line, but neither did she seek to expand the dimensions of that line.

There is a thriving motivational industry of speakers, coaches, seminars, and retreats directed towards these full time real estate sales people with a common theme of "how to get your client to say YES!" There is also a large tributary of "how to get more clients" seminars that flows back to the main river of sales magic. It will be illuminating for you to do a Google search for yourself and see what you find. What seems to be lacking is a full spectrum of instruction on "how to actually do a great job for your client."

Finally, there are those real estate professionals that embrace the confirmation of the fiduciary responsibility. Instead of a two dimensional line that is not to be crossed, they respectfully accept the invitation to enter the three dimensional domain of their client's best interests. They ask questions until the goals are defined, compose the schedule to achieve said goals, and seek out the relevant data for all the decisions that will be required along the way to those goals at the optimum time. They revere the space in which their clients can make good decisions because they understand that it is sacred.

Where the Ascot's agent handled arising issues in the marketing and selling of their home in a reactive or passive manner, the real estate professional would have sought to bring as many of those issues to the Ascots for their consideration at the optimum time in a proactive manner. We saw earlier that many of the physical issues that occurred during the Buyer's inspections could have not only been anticipated, but also discussed and defined to give the Sellers the opportunity to make a good decision at an ideal time. Not one issue is unique to the two potential paths- passive and proactive- only the time at which those decisions are made, and how much time there is to make them.

Chapter

6

Middle Preparation

So far, we have looked at length at what would be considered "The Beginning" of selling a home, from reviewing written records of the property and taking the first tour, through to completion of disclosures and inspections. I hope I have successfully made the argument for the listing agent to invest in proactive actions for the benefit of their client, prior to placing said client's home on the market. Let's move now in a more linear fashion through those activities I define as "The Middle" and "The End" of the process of selling a home. Outlined, these phases include:

The Middle: Preparation and Execution
Photography
Copy
Unveiling
Showing
Negotiation

The End: Management
Escrow
Contingencies
Closing

The Middle, Part One: Preparation

I know it sounds like something your grandmother said to you as a teenager, but it is true- first impressions matter. A property only has one opportunity to create an attractive first impression in the marketplace. That very first critical look by all the relevant eyes of potential "A" Buyers (and their agents) is by far the most important of this process.

And how does that first look occur? Usually via a small picture on a phone, tablet, or computer. That first glimpse is a critical unveiling with only one of two possible outcomes: the viewer is interested and seeks more information, or the viewer is unmoved to pursue the property. This being the case, I use the word "unveil" quite purposefully. Why not control the event in which that first important glimpse takes place? Make it an event that relevant eyes are excited to attend and then, most important of all, deliver. The entire "Middle" of the real estate process is about delivering the property at its best to attract its best Buyers. By this point, we have decided the best price for the subject property, as well as the best manner in which to physically present the house to the market. Now, we begin this second phase of getting all of those things done.

I find it best to start by assigning the tasks that need to be completed, and then putting those tasks on the calendar. For the Seller, it usually means committing to the date by which they will pack and move anything currently in the property that will not be used in showing off the property in its best light. Any painting, repairs, upgrades, and staging are scheduled and managed through completion until the client's home is camera ready.

Photography

The entire exercise of visually strengthening the presentation of the subject home is going to be captured- for better or for worse- in its photography. Yes, the eventual Buyer or Buyers will walk the property, but their first impression, and more importantly, their decision to further pursue or pass, will be almost solely based on their immediate response to the first picture they see. If that does not scare you, then you do not yet grasp what is at stake with the photography of a home.

I see homes presented to the market every day with terrible photographs. I have seen exterior photos of a home shot from the listing agent's car with the driver's side door window framing the shot. This same agent wants to make thousands of dollars through the sale of that home, but cannot even get out of his car to take a photograph? There is at least one website dedicated to the unfortunate pictures agents have used to represent their properties- and funny as it might be for the general public, it is incredibly sad for the Owner of that property. I am amazed by how little some agents are willing to do for the commission they demand.

Since photography is a very valuable tool in the marketing of a property, I am always willing to pay a premium for premium results. But the listing agent needs to do more than just hire a good photographer to go out and take some pretty shots of a property. It is the agent's job to know the goal of the photo shoot. How are you trying to present this home to the marketplace? What is the thesis statement of this particular home that you wish to communicate to the marketplace as clearly as possible? How are you positioning this home in the mind's eye of the pool of Buyers that you wish to attract? These are the basic, Marketing 101-style questions that need to be answered by the listing agent first, so that the presentation of the property in all its forms – pricing, physical presentation, visual media – are executed to provide those answers.

Car ads are a great example of product photography with which we are all familiar. The company that won the competitive bid for a particular ad campaign of a specific vehicle knows who the car company wants to attract to the subject vehicle and how different subsets of Buyers are typically motivated to purchase a car. This company cleverly designs their ad to have a real effect on their intended audience. They certainly do not just send some random photographer over to a car lot to take some photos. No, they design the best environment in which to shoot this vehicle: the best lighting, best angle, best color, and so many other specific decisions in presenting their argument to implant in their targeted audience the desire to purchase this vehicle.

Similarly, a listing agent needs to clearly state how he or she intends to position a home in the marketplace to attract that subset of "A" Buyers to that home in a manner that they will compete to purchase that home. What is your thesis statement to the market?

"This is a rare, preserved, large post and beam home in a great school district."

This was the thesis statement for a home I represented in 2010. It was a one-owner split level Post and Beam home on a tiered lot in a good neighborhood with good schools. Up a steep driveway, it did not show its strengths from the street, but inside there was a surprising view of downtown Los Angeles, and the elevated rear yard was another pleasant surprise. With a large pool of creative entertainment industry people in the area, I felt this home would attract a creative couple that had school age children and were hoping to find a cool, architectural home in a good school district, which is not a common combination.

Prior to photography, we decluttered the home, in order to best showcase its architectural details. We trimmed the landscaping to show off the view. We decided not to complete any interior upgrades that would lessen the original provenance of the architecture. We rented some period furniture to highlight its unique style, and in the ad copy, I highlighted that the Seller is the original owner/builder of this home, which enhanced the message of it still remaining in its original condition. Like selling a vintage 1965 Mustang, the more original, the more valuable it is to the lover of that car.

The direction to the photographer was specific with regards to the front of the home "black and white to look as if shot in 1962". For the interior shots, we focused on the rooms that best highlighted the original architectural style, including the living room, family room, and master bedroom with wide angles that captured the preserved wood floors, posts, and wood ceilings, as well as the floor-to-ceiling windows. In the dining room we focused on the one of a kind dining room table, which had been designed by the home's architect specifically for this space when the home was built. The yard photographs all highlighted the views and the privacy of this parcel.

Through our efforts, we gave the targeted pool of Buyers the shots we had determined would be most valuable to them. This is a distinctly different approach than merely cataloguing the home in a series of stills so the Buyer could "tour" through the property on their phone or computer. That may be appropriate for insurance purposes, but not for telling the visual story we sought to broadcast. Our photos were meant to peak enough interest to draw our targeted Buyers to the property, as well as to re-confirm their desire for the property once they had actually made the time to walk through it with their agent. And it worked! We attracted a brilliant couple working in "the industry" who had growing twins. The husband even had a doctorate in architecture. The home had found its audience; they competed for it and purchased it gladly for a premium.

However, there is an important difference between photos that show off a property in its best light and photos that do not reflect the property that the potential Buyer experiences when they get there. Pictures absolutely can lie, and all too often do, in real estate marketing. But to what end? Photoshopping out large power lines in the rear yard does not make those power lines disappear when the Buyer arrives to see the home in person. Rather than increase their interest, the potential Buyer who is left to discover that a home looks nothing like the photos that peaked their interest will feel manipulated, likely negating any interest they may have had in the property. It is therefore vital that your photos truthfully represent the property. The photos can either begin to build the chain of decisions that lead to purchasing a home or not. Poor photos fail to cause a potential Buyer to begin to pursue a home further. Pictures that are attractive, but not true, will attract Buyers, only to break that first link of interest and terminate the decision chain.

Good photography is not an accident, and it can only be produced by good photographers. Your agent should be willing to pay for a good photographer. It is some of the best money spent in marketing a home. A good residential photographer must have both talent and skill, but they also need to work cooperatively with the agent and the Owner. The best one I know shows up on time, is respectful of the client's home, listens to my goals, and is willing to share his own ideas as well. He is also willing to provide options. I have never used all of the shots he has provided me on a given property, but I am always thankful for the options he provides. Pay your photographer well for good work, and pay him/her promptly.

I have purposely used the above example from 2010 as it will seem like a bygone era to many agents in the marketplace today. Now, agents can use a wide variety tools in their visual presentation of a home, including drones, videos, 3D floor plans and the like. I strongly encourage the use of any and all tools that will do the best job of telling the visual story of a given property. I just want to add the obvious truth that just because a tool is available does not make it the right tool to market a specific property. I have seen countless drone shots looking down on the roofs of homes on the market that are more repelling than compelling. As I write this, there is a home in my area with a 3D floor plan of a two bedroom home incorporated into its advertising. I love that the agent is willing to pay for this creative tool in the marketing of this property, but this particular tool is only serving to highlight the most limiting feature of this property- that one of the bedrooms is on the first floor, while the other is in the basement. The location, the large lot, the view, the tasteful upgrades- the property has so many strengths worth showing off to the market, making the high tech highlighting of the weak floor plan a non-strategic choice of visual media. The progress made in the number of tools available to agents in their visual presentation of homes simply increases the need for those agents to use them wisely.

Copy

"A true post and beam home is a work of art. With its open floor plan, exposed wood beams, and walls of glass it feels like a sculpture in which one is graced to live. The original vision of architects Hawkins and Lindsey has been meticulously maintained by the original Owner since she commissioned its construction in 1962 on these two view lots in Glendale's sought after Montecito Park neighborhood."

Pictures alone can tell a story. In fact, I think that the same set of pictures can tell any number of stories to any number of people. But marketing a home means choosing, and then committing to, the story you want to tell. Good real estate copy (I sense your doubt that those four words have ever been used before in that particular arrangement) tells a specific story. The copy above was the first paragraph of the final copy I used in marketing the large post and beam home referred to in preceding photography section. That particular home had the most sought-after character in that art minded pool of Buyers whose business we were seeking. The second sentence of the copy not only highlights the fundamental traits in this prized style, but draws attention to the fact that the property is in its most valuable original condition. The third sentence provides the reason this piece of art has been so preserved, and then highlights the rarity, and thus the added value, of finding this home in a neighborhood known for good schools, while the mention of the view provides the best support for the argument that this rare find is worth the premium being asked.

I do not claim it as an example of good prose, but it does, clearly and precisely, tell the story we wanted to tell. Most real estate copy is akin to some sort of cheap vanilla icing that agents slap on their advertising to call it a finished cake. "Trite" is too trite to describe most real estate ad copy: *charming traditional on a charming street in an absolutely charming neighborhood.*

Again, I am not saying that you have to be a skilled writer to compose good copy. My SAT verbal scores show that I am not blessed with a writer's aptitude. But it is undoubtedly worth all of the effort to be intentional in choosing what you want to say about a property, and then attempting to do so. We all have the aptitude to do just this, whether the words flow easily from our minds, or, as in my case, have to be painfully mined. For me, composing copy is one of the most difficult tasks I do for my clients.

Of course, not all marketable narratives are as obvious as the one about the unique, one owner, post and beam with a view. In truth, most properties sit in neighborhoods with many other similar homes surrounding them. What story can be told that has not already been told several times over in this neighborhood?

Let's return again to that "average" evaluation example we reviewed earlier, which ended up selling for $885,000. It is two doors away from a home that was designed by a famous architect, and there are several other homes on the street that are much more noticeable architecturally. Frankly, I believe this particular home was one of the last to be built on this road, because there is not much flat land on the lot; most of the rear yard is an upslope. The design of this home is a challenge to categorize. On the outside, it is more traditional for the neighborhood with lines like a "Gregg-built" home- a local builder that was active in this neighborhood for decades. The floor-plan is common for this builder as well but the design and finishes are more mid-century in their leanings. In looking again at the first permit pulled for this home in 1954, I noticed that the original builder was scratched out with another builder handwritten on that permit in the city records. The scratched-out builder was Webster Wiley. I have no idea why this builder was scratched out and no way of finding out, but he is known locally for some very characteristic mid-century homes, not so much in this immediate neighborhood, but within the same city. It's as if the original owner was going to build a modest traditional home on the last lot on this nice street, but was influenced by the cutting-edge modern home that had been built just two parcels away. The result is an interesting synthesis of traditional and modern designs.

Here is the first paragraph from the very rough second draft:

In 1954 Julius Shultz selected this parcel on Glendale's iconic Niodrara Drive on which to build his dream home. With Shindler's stunning Rodriguez House already well established just two doors away, Mr. Shultz must have been influenced to blend the best of traditional with more modern design. The result is this clever synthesis with traditional exterior lines in combination with mid-century leanings throughout the interior.

It's rough, but try not get hung up on the state of this early draft. Notice what I am trying to get on paper about the house: its location on a great street, and that the blend of designs is purposeful with some cachet from a well-known home nearby.

I am actually a little embarrassed to have shown you this rough copy, but the process is getting the gist of your thoughts out in an initial rough draft. Only then can brutal editing and hopeful refining begin. The second rough paragraph:

The entry opens to the large formal living room with original hardwood flooring, blank ity blank, and a warm fireplace hearth. The oversized formal dining room allows for grand entertaining. The kitchen has been thoughtfully updated to preserve the original culinary DNA as well as please the demanding household chef. The central hall leads to all three bedrooms. The two baths have been painstakingly preserved to protect the pristine blankety blank tile.

Yikes, that is rough, but I have a skeleton to work off of while I search for the details I want to highlight. I was suspicious that the bathroom tiles (which are not something I would typically highlight) would be the best and most valuable evidence of this purposeful synthesis I was attempting to convey, but hopefully, the pool of Buyers that we hope to have competing for this property will think these tiles are very cool, rather than just old, if I can correctly identify them as such.

The rear yard was the most surprising positive feature of this property. Because of the upslope in the rear yard, the rear patio represented most of the "useful" portion of the back yard. But one of the Owners was a trained and gifted landscape designer. She transformed the hill in the back yard into a gorgeous retreat with a path winding up the hill through pampered gardens, shade trees, and fruit trees. The best part was that she designed and built two destinations at the top of the hill- one with a view deck where four people could enjoy dinner after sunset, and the other a small contemplative sitting area for two. The hill was no longer viewed as a negative in comparison to a flat yard, but now a positive.

The Owners also transformed their rear patio by designing and building an outdoor family room. With their work on the hill as well as the patio, I was able present the rear yard as a positive, though not common, feature of this property.

In 1954 Julius Shultz selected this parcel on Glendale's iconic Niodrara Drive on which to build. With Rudolph Shindler's famous Rodriguez House already well established just two doors away, Mr. Shultz must have been inspired to blend the best of traditional with more modern design. The result is this savvy synthesis with traditional exterior lines in concert with mid-century leanings throughout the interior.

The flowing floor plan allows for ease of fine living within this well-conceived design. The entry opens to the formal living room with hardwood flooring, original corner casement windows, and a warm fireplace hearth. There is elegant entertaining in the oversized formal dining room with its view out to the lush gardens. The household chef will thrive in the tastefully updated kitchen. All three bedrooms are off the central hall. Notice the pristine mid-century tiles that have been preserved in both baths- they look like vintage Gladding McBean Hermosa Tiles that were produced locally at that time.

It's the rear grounds where the Owners have shown off their vision and talents. The free standing open-air family room is just genius for LA living- enjoying the big screen with hardwired sound in the gorgeous natural setting. The rear yard has been professionally conceived and lovingly tended- you will be rewarded if you follow the path through the pampered gardens and fruit trees to the romantic view deck near the top. The home also has central heat and air, an updated electrical service, a new driveway, and a two-car attached garage with ample storage and an additional wood working room.

The Middle: Execution

Unveiling

Together, we have determined the market value of the property, chosen just the right asking price to yield the highest selling price, conducted our inspections, and completed the list of repairs decided upon. We are now, finally, ready to move forward with bringing the property onto the market; or, as I prefer to call it, we are now prepared to "unveil" the property to the marketplace. I use the word "unveil" quite purposefully to describe how we intend to introduce a subject property to the market. For our purposes, I am defining "going on the market" as when the listing agent uploads all of the necessary information into an agents-only service that is regulated by the real estate agent community. This system is referred to as the Multiple Listing Service, or, more commonly, the MLS as it will be referred to hereafter.

We are all familiar with unveilings as they are represented in the movies. There is a large sculpture loosely wrapped in a massive swath of fabric, surrounded by a crowd of influential arts patrons who first gasp and then applaud as the great artist's latest work is dramatically revealed. Being this imaginary wealthy art patron, I imagine that my presence would be in demand for art shows of this nature, and I would likely receive all kinds of invitations to such unveiling events. Some would interest me and some would not. Why keep sending me these expensive invitations to Andy Warhol exhibits, when it is known that I like all things impressionistic, while my wife cannot miss an event featuring Chinese ceramics? Even in this silly imagination of me being a wealthy collector of art, it is obvious that it takes some stimulus to get me to a specific exhibit. Someone smart would have taken note of what I am interested in and what I will make time to see, and then invited me to something which they believe I will find intriguing.

If we think of a home heading for the market as a new work of art, the most discerning next step is to attract those who are most interested in its type. Then, with a dramatic reveal of the piece to its most adoring patrons, we can invite them to bid competitively to acquire it. We should therefore be looking for the best ways to attract these patrons to a specific home. We have already carefully crafted the specific visual presentation of the home in its best light, and the most relevant narration to tell a specific story to a specific subset of the Buyer's pool. But now, how do we get the invitations to the right patrons? What is the mechanism to do this in real estate?

This may seem like an old-fashioned answer, but the best way to get the best patrons to your property is still to go through real estate agents. I know it sounds self-serving, as I have been an active agent for over 30 years, but with that admitted bias, I ask you to consider the following. Let's imagine a very gifted networker that really has the attention of thousands of relevant eyeballs within the active pool of Buyers. This one very gifted networker could boast a much larger network than any other individual networker. Let's even imagine that this especially gifted networker somehow controlled 10%, 20%, or even 50% of the market- which would be amazing. If this master networker were a real estate agent, real estate company, or real estate site, they would most likely boast that they can directly contact more Buyers than any other single agent in the marketplace, and that may be true. But recall, if you will, what kind of Buyer we are trying to attract to our property. We are trying to connect with those Buyers that have had the benefit of working with an agent for some time. We are looking for Buyers whose agent has taught them about the local market, shown them several properties in the local market, and assisted them in getting financially prepared by sourcing their down payment and getting them pre-approved for a loan. If these "A" Buyers are the very Buyers we want to attract, then marketing to the agents is effectively marketing to a majority of those best prepared Buyers. If a network were pictured like a leaf or perhaps a branch, one entity could claim to have the attention of the largest branch, but by marketing to the all of the agents, you market to the full collection of networks in the market – all those leaves and branches composing the whole tree and even the entire forest. It is a simple mathematical proof: the sum of the many networks is greater than the sum of even the largest individual network.

When hired to market a property, I am often asked by the Seller if I have a Buyer for their home. The answer is often

"Yes, but." I explain to the Sellers that "it would seem an odd coincidence that I happen to know the very best Buyer for your home out of all of the Buyers in the current pool." If the goal is to sell my client's home for the highest price with the best terms, does it not make sense to expose that home to the entire marketplace?

This current high cycle of the residential real estate market, which began in 2015 and has lasted well into 2019, is so hot that I routinely receive multiple offers on nearly every property that I market. The Buyers in this kind of market by necessity must compete with several other Buyers on the most desirable properties, and they are naturally seeking ways to increase their chances of being selected by the Seller. One unfortunate by-product of this kind of market is that many Buyers currently believe that if they allow the property's listing agent to represent them, they will have a greater chance of getting the property. Why? They believe that if the listing agent is getting all of the commission rather than splitting it with another agent, the listing agent will be financially motivated to get their offer accepted. You are right to likely see an obvious problem- the listing agent already has a fiduciary responsibility to the Seller which includes assisting the Seller in selecting the Buyer that is truly the best choice for that Seller. As soon as the listing agent allows a larger commission check to influence the Seller's choice of Buyers, that listing agent has compromised their fiduciary responsibilities to the Seller.

In this current hot market in which homes are selling quickly, I see listing agents that appear to be making marketing choices for their own benefit rather than that of their clients. Buyers sense that the sooner they can have access to a listing the better chance they have of winning the competition for that property, or even avoiding that competition altogether. I am constantly asked by agents and Buyers "Do you have any listings coming up?" My pat answer is "Yes, I always have something coming up." They usually pursue a bit further in hopes of early access to this listing and the chance of securing it "off market." I do not blame the Buyer's agents for doing this- they are just working hard for their clients. However, the listing agent must consider a vital question: Why would a non-competitive process be better for the Seller?

There certainly can be benefits to an "off market" sale for a Seller. If the Seller perceives the marketing process of their own home as too stressful or invasive, they may be willing to give up maximizing their sale price in exchange for a perceived lower stress transaction. It being the Seller's property, they have every right to make such a decision. In my 30+ years of representing Sellers, I have had four Sellers make an informed decision about not marketing their home to the full market place and instead choosing to sell their home "off market." In these few cases, I made it clear that they would sell for a higher price if they went on the market, but they made the decision not to and I believe it was the right decision for them. But for most of us, the perceived stress of allowing our homes to go on the market (and there is real stress involved) is worth knowing the eventual sales price and terms were the highest and best possible.

A listing agent can also entice a Buyer to pay above the market price of a listing in exchange for the Buyer not having to go through the process of competing for the property. In other words, the Buyer is given an opportunity to pay a premium for a home in exchange for not going through the stress of potentially competing in a multiple offers scenario. This can be an effective tool for a listing agent to utilize in fulfilling their fiduciary responsibility for the Seller, but again I must point out the odd coincidence that a listing agent happens to know the one Buyer out of the entire pool of Buyers that would pay the most for this particular property. This certainly would seem to be the exception to the rule with a rather small mathematical probability. Remember, no matter how large the individual master networker branch, it is not larger than the tree, and certainly not bigger than the entire forest.

Allow me to propose another metaphor. If the market comprises the entire pool of Buyers, each individual agent has a fishing pole- but all of the agents together would comprise a significantly larger net. It seems clear that the fiduciary responsibility of the listing agent compels them to market their client's property beyond their own network of Buyers and out to the all of the real estate agents who are in turn connected collectively with a majority of the pool of Buyers.

There are those agents in any given area that have earned the dubious reputation of marketing their clients' homes in a manner that yields a rather high percentage of transactions in which they also represent the Buyer. I am in no way saying that an agent cannot fulfill their fiduciary responsibilities to their clients while acting as a dual agent. There are certainly times when the listing agent's diligence on behalf of the Seller does directly attract the best Buyer for that particular property from their own network. I am only pointing out that statistics would seem to show that this should occur in a rather smaller percentage of listings that a particular listing agent sells. Problems can arise when a listing agent's marketing choices are designed to increase the probability of that agent also representing the Buyer for that property. This can be done by pricing a home too high, so that the pool of "A" Buyers will not pursue the property and the listing agent's Buyer client can negotiate a lower price. A self-interested listing agent can also inhibit other agents from showing the property, which clearly limits the property's exposure to other agent's Buyer networks. A listing agent can even post poor quality pictures online so that other agents are less compelled to show it to their clients. At best, all of these actions can simply be poor marketing due to laziness, error, or inexperience. At worst, the listing agent has violated the sacred ground of their fiduciary responsibilities. Whatever the reason, the Owner of the property suffers a lower eventual sale price, while the listing agent is oddly rewarded for representing the eventual Buyer and making a larger commission. Life is too short for any sort of prospering from poor performance.

Let us return to the unveiling of a property to the market. We want to create an event for the best patrons of our art to attend. In the areas that I work, the local real estate associations host weekly caravans of the new properties to the market. This commitment of organized time each week for local agents to devote solely to seeing the newest listings on the market is an invaluable marketing opportunity. We are so fortunate as to be able to predict exactly when we will have the opportunity to attract of lot of relevant networkers to our specific property.

I have found this broker caravan day to be the best day in a given week to unveil my client's listings to the marketplace. To do so, I place the home on the MLS five days prior to that caravan date with the clear instruction that there will be no showings of the property until the caravan day. This creates a short and very valuable period of time in which agents and their clients can view the property online prior to actually being able to see the property in person. This strategy accomplishes two very important goals in the beginning of our marketing campaign. The first is carving out time for demand to build. If the home were immediately available, very motivated clients would begin to see the property as soon as their schedules allow. For example, we might have two showings the next day and each of the days that follow. These Buyers would experience the property by themselves at different times of the day. But having to wait a few days for the house to be available allows more Buyers to schedule being at the property when it is available, during the broker's open house. This means the Seller can actually schedule when the most concentrated number of "A" Buyers are going to be viewing their property, and therefore, be the most prepared for the most important showings of their home. Furthermore, from a practical standpoint, it is difficult for clients to live in a house when it is for sale. In this case, maximum effort can be applied to maximum benefit.

What used to be just a practical way for agents to see a lot of new listings in a short period of time has become for me the most important day of marketing my client's property. I treat it as a party for agents and their clients to come and see this great new listing in its very best condition. Everything is just so- the kind of put together you like your own home to be when guests are coming over. For years I have served lunch during these broker's open houses. Of all the homes that an agent could see on that day, I want them to always think mine will be worth seeing- not only will it look great and be priced intelligently, but I am present if they have any questions or requests, and they get a free lunch to boot. Also, I get the added benefit of reading the immediate reaction of several agents and their clients to the property, which proves invaluable moving forward in the marketing campaign.

The second benefit of this lag period between posting a listing online and scheduling its first unveiling is that it clearly demonstrates to the agents and their clients that the sale of this property is going to be happening in a competitive but fair manner. A Seller may be tempted to say here, "What do I care about the process being fair as long as I get the highest price?" The simple truth is that a fair process is good business in that it yields the highest result. Buyers and their Agents are extremely sensitive to the actions of the listing agent. If it appears that the listing agent is marketing the property in a way that will more likely lead to the listing agent also representing the eventual Buyer, the pool of Buyers and their agents are less motivated to pursue the property with their very best offer. Why? If they think the process is in any way rigged against them, they would rather not even try. The emotional roller coaster a Buyer must ride when deciding to pursue a house takes a great emotional toll, from scheduling initial showings in an already busy schedule, to reaching a decision with their significant others, to reviewing real estate forms, and coordinating with their Lender, all the while fearing that other Buyers may get there first. Most people who are fortunate enough to be in a position to make an offer on a home are doing so by working very hard in their daily lives. The added work of attempting to purchase a home in an already full schedule takes extra time and extra effort in a schedule that is usually out of an extra anything.

So how does the listing agent acting in a fair manner benefit the Seller as well as the Buyer? For the Seller, they know that the eventual Buyer was the absolute best their home attracted out of the entire pool of Buyers. For the Buyer in a competitive market like today, if they are confident the process will be fair and they know the Seller's decision will be based on the best price and terms, they are more inclined to compete at their highest level for their desired home.

On the other hand, if the Buyers and their agents do not believe the listing agent is acting fairly, they hesitate to move forward. This is a real example that I have witnessed. An agent in my office was representing a very qualified and motivated Buyer. He had worked with her long enough that she was an absolutely prepared "A" Buyer. On a Monday, that agent noted that a new listing had just been posted on the MLS. The agent in my office called the property's listing agent and was informed that there would be no showings until the caravan on the coming Wednesday. The Buyer's agent shared the information with his client and they excitedly agreed to see the property together during that Wednesday's scheduled caravan. Touring the property that Wednesday confirmed the Buyer's decision to pursue purchasing this property, so much so that the Buyer informed their agent that they would be willing to go well over the asking price to get this home.

That same Wednesday, the Buyer's agent called the listing agent to inform him that he had a very interested client and to inquire as to when the Seller would be looking at offers. He called several times but did not get a call back from the listing agent that day. The next day, Thursday, the listing agent called the agent in my office back to inform him that the Seller had accepted an offer the evening before, and that the property was no longer available. Do you understand? Me neither.

Why would the Seller have their home placed on the market, attract Buyers, and then truncate the process in which Buyers could compete for it? Yes, there is the possibility that the chosen Buyer saw it that same Wednesday morning, made an offer, and the Seller believed it would be the best offer that any Buyer would make. But this seems a bit incredible, especially since this other Buyer's agent informed the listing agent that he had a client ready to make a very good offer if only the listing agent would inform him about the schedule in which the Seller would review offers. Here I must add that the Seller has the right to accept an offer when they choose to do so, but does this seem logical given the clear existence of another very motivated Buyer? Well, when escrow closed a month later, it was clear that the listing agent that represented the Seller also represented the Buyer. Hmmm...

The emotional energy expended by my agent's client was massive. To have found the home she had worked so hard for and had hoped to secure for her family, only to be told they were somehow too late when they had strictly adhered to the listing agent's instructions, was devastating. That Buyer, that agent, as well as others that were interested in that property will be very wary to pursue a property brought to market by that listing agent again. Therefore, it appears as if the listing agent's actions will not only short change the Seller of that property, but subsequent Sellers represented by that agent as well.

Do you now see why projecting a fair process is so important? It is not only the right thing to do, it is simply good business. Remember Maximus' words to his cavalry before the first battle in Gladiator: "What we do here, echoes in eternity." The marketplace is certainly not eternity, but the echoes of our actions can be heard clearly within it.

Showings

Once we have successfully unveiled the property to the marketplace (with a gap leading up to the first open house for the brokers/agents and their clients), we begin the period when agents will actually be allowed to bring their clients to and through the property. From the homeowner's perspective, there are just two tasks to concentrate on during the showing period. The first is invitation- we must make it easy for agents and their clients to see the property. Since the goal is to attract the greatest subset of the relevant Buyers pool to our property in the shortest amount of time, it is critical to not inhibit the flow of "A" Buyers to and through the property. This likely sounds elementary, but it is worth discussing, since most of us are still living within the home we are attempting to sell. This means we have to coordinate our daily lives of homework, eating, bathing, exercising, and the many details of getting kids ready for all of their activities, while keeping the house in pristine condition for prospective Buyers. This is neither an easy nor a fun task. The best way to handle it is to first accept that it will be demanding. Once you accept the demands of the task, then commit to them wholeheartedly. I usually recommend a daily schedule in which you can assure that the house will look pristine for agents and their Buyers. For example, if we state that the property can be shown each day between 10am and 7pm, it gives agents a predictable schedule in which they can arrange for their clients to see the property. This type of schedule allows the occupants of the house to do all they need to do within it in the evening and morning, with "show time" starting at 10am each day.

There are usually compromises to be made in coming up with a schedule like 10am to 7pm. It is difficult for most to be preparing their normal dinner meals starting after 7pm, especially if you like to steam Brussel sprouts and broccoli with your nightly fish dinner. These meals can taste delicious, but the odor can undo all the work you have done to attract a great Buyer to your home. Remember how you would prepare your home before guests come over, would you want them to be greeted by a wall of fish and broccoli stink? More often than cooking, it is the family pet that presents the greatest obstacles. As pet owners, we become accustomed and oblivious to their effect on Buyers walking through our home. Just inside your front door, the Buyers and their agents can sense if you have a dog or cat. They also sense the odor of other pets, like birds, reptiles, and guinea pigs- they may not be as certain as to exactly what they are, but they are certain that they are there. I can unequivocally tell you that this is not a good thing. There is not a Buyer who walks in and says, "Oh, I love that sweet smell of wet dog in this house!" Just be honest. Know how your house smells and deal with it for the time your home is on the market. Remember, anything that affects just one percentage of the eventual sales price is significant- and persistent odors definitely do.

If you smoke in your home, you are lowering its value by several percent. I grew up with two parents that smoked in the house. It was not until I was in high school that I realized I smelled like an ashtray wherever I went. It was in my hair, my clothes, my shoes, and I did not even smoke. The response of a Buyer is immediate and quite negative to the smell of smoke. They know there is no inexpensive solution to removing that smell if they purchase your property. Enough said.

You have worked hard to get your house in showing shape. It is now critical to maintain that showing shape throughout the marketing period of your home. Maintain your presentation.

Do not forget to discuss and decide upon the method by which agents will schedule their showing of the property, especially by determining who the agent will contact to set up and confirm an appointment. Do not make the Buyers' agents have to hunt around just to schedule an appointment. Give them one easy contact (phone, text, email) for the chosen contact person. That chosen contact person will respond to all of those contacts quickly and make the Seller aware of the scheduled appointment in a timely manner.

Different areas have different methods for granting access to their properties for showings, falling broadly into two methods of actual access: allowing the use of a lock box for a key to the property, or not allowing the use of a lock box. Whatever the system, the listing agent and the Seller need to establish how showings will be scheduled, and when they can have access to the property. You do not want to experience that worst-case scenario where the Seller is in the shower and a Buyer walks in...trust me, it is never a good thing.

Here a quick word about "those agents." Most agents really do try to remain respectful of a Seller's home while they are showing it and will follow the schedule for showings that the listing agent has posted for them on their MLS. Unfortunately, there are always those few who seem to live life in a bubble, oblivious to their effect on others. These few will say rude things in earshot of a Seller about their home. They will show up unannounced for a "showing" and boldly lie that they got permission from the listing agent, or they will walk through the garden and trample flowers. These few do not seem to remain in real estate for long, but there always seems to be a fresh supply of these few immature agents. It is best to know before you place your home on the market that you may encounter one of these few miserable people- do not let it bother you. They are just a temporary nuisance and ultimately irrelevant to the sale of your home.

The Seller can expect to experience some anxiety while the house is on the market and available for showings. After all the hard work of preparing for potential Buyers to view their home, the Seller naturally wants positive feedback about what agents and their clients think of the house. They want to know how the market is reacting to their home and it is the listing agent's job to provide them this information based upon the potential Buyer's agent's reactions to the house. Do the agents think it is priced well? Are the agents bringing up negative attributes of the house that had not been pre-identified by the listing agent? Are the agents scheduling showings? And how are the Buyers reacting during those showings? How many showings are taking place? Are they all different Buyers or are some Buyers seeing the property multiple times? This is all the type of market feedback the Sellers can use to gauge how the market is reacting to their home. If there has only been one showing in the first week on the market as compared to ten showings, this is very different, but relevant information for the listing agent and the Seller.

The successful marketing of a home requires openness to this constant feedback. When this feedback is positive, it confirms the decisions made thus far by the Seller. When the feedback is negative, it may challenge the decisions made thus far. This in no way means that those decisions are incorrect, but continued negative feedback from the marketplace does provide the Seller the opportunity to re-visit them. Are we priced correctly? Are there floor plan issues we have not addressed properly? Is the market as a whole slowing down? These and others are relevant questions to consider throughout the marketing process. Not being willing to consider negative market feedback only adds time and subtracts money from the Sellers realized net proceeds. No company prospers that is not keenly interested in the feedback of the market for their product, goods and/or services.

Positive feedback is informative as well. If there are twelve showings of a home within the first few days of it being on the market, the Seller knows that their property is attracting the Buyers they were hoping to attract. If some of those Buyers make offers within the first week at asking price or above, the Seller can be encouraged that their property is going to sell above what they were asking for it. When blessed with multiple offers, the Seller is given very clear information from the marketplace. If there are five offers with two just below asking, one at asking, and two more a little over asking, the market clearly believes your property is worth what you are asking and perhaps a bit more. If there are multiple offers and all are well under the asking price, then the Seller has a clear market impression that the property is desirable, but perhaps not worth what is being asked. Lastly, if there are several offers well above asking price, then the market is indicating that the eventual Buyer that is selected by the Seller may pay significantly more than the asking price. Market feedback is clearly critical information for the listing agent to disclose to the Seller, as it provides them with real time data and context in this developing decision-making process.

Naturally, multiple offers are always fun for the Seller and the Listing Agent, but how about when the offers are not coming in? The Seller and their agent should establish prior to marketing a home how often they will meet to review their chosen marketing strategy while the property is available. For approximately the first twenty five years of my career, I would schedule a formal in-person meeting with the Seller if their home was not under contract after being on the market for thirty days. The thinking was that thirty days was a good estimate of the cycle in which we unveiled their property to the market and could expect that the relevant eyeballs saw the property and decided to pursue or not pursue. That timeframe does not fit the current market; in my area, a listing is considered middle-aged if it does not have an offer in the first two weeks, and ancient after just thirty days.

Today, I need to pre-schedule that meeting (which I frankly hope to not have to have) for two weeks after the unveiling of a home if we are not in escrow yet. With growing "Days on Market" being a substantial negative, it is critical to have the conversation as to why a home is not in escrow after two weeks. I admit this timeframe is short, but we have to strategize our review of our marketing campaign in the context of the current sales cycle.

At that meeting, I think it is helpful to review what homes, if any, in our price range and area have gone under contract in the timeframe we have been on the market. This shows us what our hoped-for Buyers are choosing instead of the subject property. We also need to know if other homes in our price range and area have been added to the market since our unveiling, as well as if there have been any price reductions. In other words, we have to remain aware of the competition and the place of the home we are selling within its relevant marketplace.

The information is not always conclusive. Sometimes the residential real estate market just seems to take a break without explanation. There really can just be a lull. But there are many instances where a change has taken place and action is warranted. In 2014 I had two larger homes going on the market in my neighborhood towards the end of summer. As those two clients were preparing their homes for the market that spring, I saw a significant uptick in our local market. There were about six homes of similar size that sold that spring and early summer that were about 5% above where the market indicated that they would have sold earlier that year. This seemed to indicate that my estimate of their market values were about 5% to low. When they were ready to go on the market, I counseled that we could ask about 5 to 7% higher than we had discussed earlier in the year based on those surprising sales. In both cases I encouraged the Sellers to go on the market about $100,000 higher than we had been planning, and in both cases I was proved wrong.

Both of these Sellers had done their part to prepare their homes, but after I "unveiled" their homes to the market, we did not get the multiple offers I had anticipated. In both cases we had to have those meetings to re-visit our marketing decisions. I have to admit that I was embarrassed. It is always tempting in those times to find someone or something else to blame, but that is not helpful. I had to admit that I had been incorrect in my assumption that the uptick in the market just a few months earlier would continue. It did not. The local market settled a bit and remained flat with regards to pricing through the end of the year.

After admitting to my incorrect assumption, we were left with the feedback we had received from the market. Several agents and clients had expressed how beautiful the properties were, but we did not have any offers. We had to adjust our price down the same amount that I had suggested raising it prior to marketing. Again, it is an easy conversation when I am suggesting raising the price by $100,000, but always difficult when the conversation is about lowering the asking price. The temptation is usually to adjust the price a little and "see what happens." This is death by a thousand cuts. Most action plans that include the words "see what happens" are an avoidance of the market feedback one is receiving. In both of these cases, the properties were too desirable for it to be anything other than price hindering the attraction of offers. Both needed to be reduced over $100,000 and sooner rather than later. Once we adjusted the price accordingly, the showings changed and we attracted our Buyers.

The truth I had to accept was that if we had priced those homes correctly prior to unveiling, they would have sold more quickly and likely for a higher price. The risk of going for the higher sales price, which I thought was attainable, could have cost each of my clients between $25,000 and $30,000 in net proceeds after closing their respective escrows. That always stings. I enjoy being right, but when I am not, the sooner I admit it the sooner my client can be reacting correctly to the market and accomplishing their goal of selling their home. As a listing agent, it is easy to accept too much credit for success and easier still not accept enough responsibility for failure.

In real estate, there are a lot of important details to not just manage but marshal. Mistakes will happen. I have answered the phone at 3:20pm to hear, "Craig, did you cancel our 3:00 meeting?" Panic and excuses quickly parade my thoughts, but I have to stop, apologize, and admit I just forgot. I think most people can sense an excuse and find it more bothersome than whatever action I have attempted to excuse. On the other hand, I find it a bit refreshing to hear someone take responsibility for a mistake and proceed to the remedy of that mistake sans any intervening energy spent on excuse creation and explanation. I have been doing this job a long time, which means I have made most of the possible mistakes. Once I take ownership of a mistake, I can move forward and gain that much more experience.

Negotiations

As for offers, whether they come quickly as we had hoped or take a little extra time, we have finally arrived at that point where we are dealing with a written offer from an actual Buyer for our property. It will be helpful here to circle back to a listing example I shared earlier. In discussing the importance of pricing as a marketing tool, I talked about a home that was going on the market between $819K and $839K in hopes of generating a sales price of $855K to $875K+. One week prior to placing this home on the market I spoke with an agent that had a home in the neighborhood in escrow. She shared that her client had paid close to $900,000 for a home that was a little larger and within the same neighborhood as my client's. This information was a bit surprising, and too strong an indicator to be ignored. I called my clients and asked for their permission to raise the asking price of their home from $849,000 to $859,000. I had thought the goal would be $875k, but now I felt we could get more. Remember: closed sales are a glimpse of the recent past, while current escrows are data points of the present. As an aside, one must also remember that current escrows have not yet closed and are therefore less verifiable data points. On this occasion, the agent was asking for help with comparables for their upcoming appraisal, so I considered the shared information more reliable.

I had previously thought that it was important to keep the price just under $850,000 to generate multiple offers. Now I felt the risk was lower of being under that $850k threshold with the possible reward of 2 to 3% higher sales price. I explained my thinking to the Sellers, who discussed it between themselves and then gave me permission to raise the price. My assistant had to call our printer who had already begun working on the brochure and was not too pleased, but the price change was made. We placed the property on the MLS that Friday, stating that showings would begin the following Wednesday at the broker's caravan. That caravan was quite well attended and in the subsequent four days on the market the home was shown to 15 different Buyers. At the Open House that Sunday, several agents brought their clients back for a second or even third visit. The next day we received and reviewed five offers, all above asking price. Four of the offers were within 3% of the asking price, with one outlier about 5% above asking price.

Often with multiple offers there is one or even a few that standout from the others because of price, terms, and story. By "story" I mean that the reason that Buyer is interested in this particular property just seems to make sense. For example, the Buyers are having another baby and Grandmother lives in close proximity to the subject property and will be available for babysitting. That story is often not clear at the outset, but develops through the negotiation process. On this occasion, there was an all-cash offer, but the funds were held by a parent in another country. What do we care? Perhaps this parent is just being generous and once their child selects a home they will wire the money without an issue- which could be possible. But experience tells me this parent could be waiting for their child to select a possible candidate home and place it under contract, before suddenly flying into town to inspect the candidate and exercise her inherent veto power as the source of funds. In other words, who is the real Buyer? We countered this Buyer at a higher price with the stipulation that all funds necessary to close escrow be in an account belonging only to the Buyer named on the contract within seven days of acceptance. This stipulation should help reveal the strength of the strings attached to those funds.

The outlier offer well above the other offers had its own caveat: a government backed loan program. This particular program is rarely used in the area; I have been involved with just two in thirty years. This program has its own appraisal process which the Buyer is not allowed to bypass. In other words, this Buyer can offer more than anyone else, but their government backed loan program will only allow them to pay a purchase price equal to the appraised price. In our current market that is rising, Buyers are often paying a bit more than the appraised value. This Buyer, therefore, can offer more than any other Buyer with the Seller bearing the risk of it not appraising. This government backed loan program can also take longer to complete even if the appraisal is fine. This is a risky choice for the Seller to accept.

The Sellers decided to provide each of the five potential Buyers with a Multiple Counter Offer. To the outlier, they countered higher with some penalties for delays. To the other four, they countered at about 2% less.

The following morning one of the agents called to say that his client was no longer interested in the property. This left us with three candidates in addition to the outlier.

The agent for the all cash Buyer called early that day to ask some questions about the disclosures. This a typically a good sign as it shows the Buyer is actually reading the Seller's disclosures and is interested in more details. Even more telling was the email he sent me, in which he stated that the "real" Buyer is not the daughter named on the offer but the mother who resides in another country with the money for the purchase. He stated that his "real" client could not transfer the money to the US and be placed in the account of the stated Buyer for "tax purposes." This confirmed the Sellers concerns that the "real" Buyer had not even seen the property, and that the proof of funds was a bit nebulous. This Buyer did execute the Multiple Counter Offer, but with a new counter in regards to the funds residing out of the country until 48 hours prior to the proposed close of escrow. This did not mitigate the Seller's concerns about this proposal.

The outlier Buyer did not accept the multiple counter offer, but countered with essentially the same price and terms of their original offer. In other words, this Buyer was not willing to remove the risks that their proposed financing placed upon the Seller. The secondary risk of that proposed financing was time, as that type of loan can take 30 to 60 days longer than traditional lender financing. The primary risk was still the appraisal process unique to that loan program which disallowed the Buyer from paying more for the home than its appraised value even if the Buyer were willing to do so. With the market currently on an upswing, this places all of that risk on the Seller, making this offer less palatable to them.

The other two Buyers accepted the Multiple Counter Offer as written, with one of them raising the sales price an additional $1,000. The Buyer that responded with that $1,000 raise was a local family looking to purchase specifically in this neighborhood. They had made other offers on other properties and missed out in multiple offer scenarios. They appeared quite motivated and were working with an experienced agent. I called their Lender to inquire more about their pre-approval. I was looking to discern to what depth the Lender had actually vetted his client before issuing a pre-approval. Their original offer had been presented with a pre-approval letter for a much lower loan than was necessary for this purchase. When I brought this detail to the Buyer's Agent's attention, the Lender quickly sent me a revised pre-approval for a loan amount approximately 20% higher. I was hoping to hear that there was a detailed file behind this pre-approval with reviewed documentation for income, job history, and credit. If the detail does exist, then I would like to hear about the specific loan program they are seeking and why they are a good match for it. Lenders who have completed this type of in-depth pre-approval are usually open to discussing the thoroughness of their process. Lenders who have not done this tend to respond somewhat dismissively or defensively. This Lender simply stated that he did not remember the specifics of this pre-approval, but he assured me that he only provides such written pre-approval after completing a thorough file. I informed him that his client was being considered by the Seller in a multiple offer situation and that any additional information he can share about the pre-approval would be helpful. He stated that the power was now out in his part of the office and that he could not review the file for this Buyer on his computer.

The Buyer's agent for this Buyer had not supplied proof of the funds for the down payment, which is actually common to do, especially in competitive situations such as this. Though this Buyer had executed the Multiple Counter Offer which requested this information, it had not been provided. Their home address was given on the copy of their deposit check. I looked up that address on the Multiple Listing Service and found that it had been on the market and was now in escrow. Since their offer clearly stated that their proposed offer was not contingent upon the close of escrow of their current property, I called their agent again to ask about their proof of funds as well as their current escrow. She stated that their offer was not contingent upon the close of that other escrow because that escrow was due to close the following week. Stated differently, though the source of the down payment was coming from the expected close of another escrow, it was not worth mentioning. Hmm...

The last Buyer also accepted the Seller's Multiple Counter Offer without changes. When I followed up with their Lender, she informed me that these Buyers were pre-approved. I asked the usual follow up question, "What do you do before issuing such a pre-approval?" Without hesitation she responded that she had reviewed their tax returns, had their job history, their credit, and had sourced their down payment. I inquired more about that down payment source, as it looked like a stock portfolio with over five times the amount needed for the down payment. The Lender confirmed what the Buyer had indicated: they would liquidate a minority amount of their stocks for the necessary cash. I asked the Lender again if this Buyer needed to sell their current home and she reiterated that they did not and then sent that to me in writing.

I then looked at the public record for this Buyer's current home. It has a present value of approximately $1.4M and a loan of only $625k. This seemed to confirm their stated desire to downsize, as well as adding to the story of their financial strength. Their home was not on the market, but they had already selected a good listing agent and would sell that home once they had secured the home they hoped to downsize into. This all paints a clearer picture of a Buyer that can comfortably afford the subject property and is now hoping to execute their goal of doing so. Lastly, these Buyers had not only reviewed the disclosures that I had provided them from the Seller, they had executed them and returned them with their accepted Multiple Counter Offer.

I then met with the Sellers in person to review the responses from the various Buyers. I shared with them all of the information I have shared with you. They talked amongst themselves, asked further questions of me, and then informed me of their decision. Which do you believe they chose?

You are right. They chose the Buyers who wanted to downsize. They felt that this Buyer's "story" matched what we were able to verify. To the Sellers, this Buyer just seemed the most prepared and ready to make this purchase.

Now here is something that will make your eyes roll- I represented the Buyer. I know!

The End

By this point, we have explored the intricacies and the importance of the many issues and details involved in the making of good decisions with regard to residential real estate. We started with the misfortunate adventure of the Ascots in the sale of their home, and in reviewing their transaction together in detail, found that their agent had simply not prepared them or their property for the marketplace.

With this in mind, we determined that the process of selling a home is actually quite predictive, and that there are definite steps that can be taken which allow the client to proactively consider the relevant information at the optimum time in order to make the best decisions possible before and during a transaction. We have seen how both the Seller and their property need to be prepared for going on the market. We have unpacked the subsequent marketing of that property, and the negotiation of a contract. Altogether, we have thoroughly discussed that sequence defined as the *Beginning* and the *Middle* of the sale of a home.

Now we are at the *End*. A Buyer and Seller have agreed to a purchase contract and the actual transaction is going to take place in a defined timeframe. It is in this period that even the most prepared Sellers and Buyers can still experience anxiety due to the many time sensitive tasks that comprise a typical residential sales transaction.

I experienced this type of anxiety recently, as the first of my children to get married planned her wedding last summer. It was a wonderful event as two special people dedicated themselves to each other in a meaningful ceremony and joyous celebration. But in the months leading up to that day, our family unexpectedly found themselves on a train called The Wedding Express, steaming down the track with derailment and catastrophe seemingly a daily threat. How in the world did such a celebrated event become this Mr. Toad's Wild Ride? I kept hearing that "six months is barely enough time," and quickly discovered that anything associated with the term "wedding" all of a sudden triples in price. We have hosted large parties before, but they never came even close to the casually proposed $150 per person by any venues in our neighborhood. Yes, I was that Dad who seemed so embarrassingly behind on the "normal" costs for such a "memorable day." The venue, the caterer, the floral artist, the photographer, the dress maker, all spoke a coded jargon punctuated with time and dollar signs. The chaos of the Wedding Express daily threatened my missing the sublime beauty of this timeless event in my daughter's life. The day of the wedding was quite special and memorable, but the train ride was one I would rather not repeat.

There is the threat of a similar train ride in residential real estate called the The Escrow Express, only it moves several times faster than The Wedding Express and costs hundreds of thousands, or even millions, to ride. For the unprepared it can be a harrowing ride. But if the agents involved prepare their clients accordingly, the journey ends in a successful transaction with the Seller handing over the keys to a very excited Buyer. Let's take the opportunity here to slow this journey down a bit and understand the various aspects that make up this trip. It begins once the purchase contract has been agreed to by the Seller and Buyer and ends with that happy exchange of keys.

Escrow

The purchase of a car is relatively straightforward. We go to a dealer, select a vehicle, haggle, and eventually settle on a price for said car. Simple enough. But there is that period, which I loathe, when we are waiting for the paperwork and half the day is shot before all the forms are completed and we get to drive away with that new car. What happens during that period? If we agreed to purchase the car for $50,000 with a 20% down payment, that is an oral agreement which needs to be actually written down in contract form. There is also the need for a contract with the lender for the 80% of the car we are financing, with an agreed upon interest rate and terms. That Lender wants to not only be recognized on the deed as owning a large portion of the car, but they also want proof that the Buyer of the car has adequate insurance for the car when they drive it off the lot. In other words, the car Buyer and the car Dealer reach an agreement, memorialize that agreement in a contract, and then actually complete the mechanisms of that contract that allows the Buyer's money to go to the Dealer in exchange for the car being legally transferred from the Dealer to the Buyer, while also providing the lender with written proof of that transfer of ownership, a loan contract, and proof of insurance. The dealership is the appropriate and safe place, relatively, for all of this to happen.

When a Buyer and a Seller agree upon the price for a home, the Buyer does not just show up with a suitcase full of money on the Seller's front porch. No, that Buyer and Seller need a safe place in which the actual mechanisms of the transfer of money and legal title can be completed with all the entities involved, including the Buyer's Lender, the Buyer's insurance company, the Seller's Lender or Lenders, and their insurance company, just to name a few. That safe place is called escrow.

I cannot help but think of Mike Meyer's Saturday Night Live character "Middle Age Man" who would always brag with a sideways smile that he understood how escrow works. For those who find it a bit more inscrutable, escrow is not only that safe place in which a real estate transaction takes place, but also the coordinator of the many entities involved in the actual exchange of funds for the deed, or proof of ownership, of the subject property. An analogy that helps me is to think of the purchase contract that the Buyer and Seller have agreed to as the Mathematical Function or the Computer Code, and escrow as the computer into which the variables of the agreed upon function are inputted and run as entered. No? Then think of escrow as an unbiased administrator that completes instructions agreed to by others. The Buyer is going to work with such and such Lender, so the escrow company coordinates with that chosen Lender through to the funding of that loan through escrow. Escrow in turn coordinates with the Seller's side as to grant deeds, title issues, loan and lien debt payoffs, and final distribution of the funds.

This function that escrow executes is very important, and a Seller and Buyer are wise to choose a very good escrow company and officer. Like almost any business, there are cut rate escrow companies. A good and experienced escrow officer is like a traffic controller providing me (and therefore my client) valuable feedback about potential problems. There are often challenges in escrow, and the sooner we know about them, the sooner we can work on the remedy and avoid a mid-air crash. I know this sounds a bit exaggerated but think of what is at stake for both the Seller and the Buyer during this time. The transaction represents one of the largest in which both of these parties will be involved in their lives. And the transaction is more than just money- it involves the "home" of both parties. An early warning from a bright escrow officer that the Lender "seems to be stalling" can allow an early course correction and prevent a costly cancelation of this escrow.

Since the escrow company and escrow officer at that company fulfill such an important role, how should they be chosen? Typically, it is an item that is negotiated between the Seller and Buyer. All too often I have witnessed agents suggesting that their clients work with an escrow company in which their real estate company has a financial interest, which presents, at a minimum, an apparent conflict of interest. Since the choice of the escrow company and officer is such an important one, I urge Sellers and Buyers to act diligently in this selection.

Once escrow officially "opens", the selected escrow company and officer are provided a copy of the executed purchase contract, and the clock starts running on the transaction. For this example we will use the common time of a thirty day escrow, or an escrow that opens on Day 1 after the agreement has been executed and "closes" thirty days later with a deed being recorded in the Buyer's names and the Seller receiving the agreed upon funds for said real property.

This escrow period is a busy time for both the Buyer and the Seller, but especially for the Buyer. Just as the Seller did a lot of work to prepare their home for sale, now the Buyer has to accomplish a lot in a relatively short amount of time. I think it will be helpful to walk through the escrow period using the milestones that are imbedded within the typical purchase contract for a home. Those first milestones are the contingencies that have been negotiated within the contract.

Contingencies

Contingencies are the conditional statements within a purchase contract to which both the Buyer and the Seller have agreed. We have already witnessed the Ascot's tortured experience during their Buyer's physical inspection contingency. In that sale, their Buyer agreed to pay $1,640,000 IF no substantive physical deficiencies were discovered in the property by the Buyer during inspections of the various systems. Since those inspections did indeed discover several serious physical issues, that Buyer was able to renegotiate the sales price based upon the costs to repair those physical issues. Why? Because the original purchase agreement provided the Buyer the ability to cancel that contract if their expectation of the physical condition of the Ascot's property while negotiating that original contract was substantially different from what the actual physical condition of that property was found to be. Does that not all seem subjective and vague? All the more reason for the Seller to proactively define the physical condition of their property before agreeing to a purchase contract with that Buyer. Yet, this physical inspection contingency is only one of several contingencies that can be in a purchase contract and the Seller is wise to be prepared for them all. The three most common contingencies are referred to in short as Inspection, Appraisal, and Loan.

It only makes sense that a Buyer can determine the actual condition of the house and its systems before they conclude a transaction. What if the foundation has several large cracks? What if the waste lines are leaking under the house? What if the electrical panel is wired dangerously and could cause a fire? These are conditions that are good for a Buyer to discover, inspect, and quantify the cost of remedy. It also seems fair for a Buyer to say to the Seller that they want the dangerous wiring repaired at the Seller's expense or a credit for the same cost. If the Seller is not agreeable, then the Buyer can decide whether they want to continue forward with the transaction or cancel.

In years past, the standard purchase contracts in California had language stipulating the number of days the Buyer and the Seller had in these stages of communication regarding the findings of the physical inspections and the Buyer's subsequent request(s). If the Buyer and Seller could not reach an agreement within those timeframes, then the Buyer could exercise their right to cancel.

Now, that language is removed and what is left is just the timeframe in which the Buyer has the right to unilaterally cancel the transaction as a result of the findings or to remove the physical inspection contingency. The timeframes for any contingencies are also negotiated in the purchase contract. The inspection contingency is typically between 7 and 17 days in length, starting from when the contract was agreed to in its final form. During that period the Buyer does not even have to explain their reason for canceling or provide the Seller the opportunity to remedy the findings of concern. They can just simply cancel- without even stating why! If this does not concern you as a Seller, then I have done a poor job explaining it. This is why the vetting and selecting of the Buyer is so important during negotiations. The Seller is performing a risk assessment of the potential Buyers and moving forward with the best choice of that assessment. As a Seller you want a Buyer that will use the agreed upon contingency for the stated purpose. However, one must recognize that a Buyer with a right to cancel the deal unilaterally has a significant amount of leverage. They can attempt to renegotiate the deal with the threat of backing out. If this means the Seller will have to go back on the market, it not only means wasted marketing days, but the real possibility of selling for less. But as we discussed earlier, when the Seller has completed their disclosures thoroughly, pre-inspected issues that would likely arise in a typical inspection, and shared that information with the Buyer during the negotiation of the purchase contract, the Seller greatly reduces the risk of cancelation during the physical inspection contingency.

In our standard CAR contracts, the default timeframe for the physical inspection contingency is 17 days. I believe that is usually too long. A motivated Buyer can usually schedule a general physical inspection of a given property within 5 days of acceptance. If specific issues of concern come to light in that general inspection, those issues typically can be inspected by a specific inspector (i.e. roofing contractor, HVAC contractor, masonry contractor etc.) within an additional 3 to 5 days. After that point, the Buyer should be ready to respond to the Seller with a request for repairs. Of course, there are exceptions, but I believe the Seller should have the Buyer agree to act diligently and remove contingencies as soon as possible.

The inspection contingency is usually the most emotional in a transaction. For a Seller, the home that they have lived in is now being scrutinized by a series of "experts" paid for by the Buyer with the fear of financial loss, renegotiation, or cancelation. For the Buyer, they are now being shown all of the imperfections of the property that they were hoping would be their future home, which creates fear of additional costs and safety concerns. A Buyer is likely to act in one of three ways during the contingency period: fair, unreasonable, or unfair.

Most properly selected Buyers will respond in a fair manner to the results of the inspection. I say this with the observation that most people respond in a fair manner when they are treated fairly. In our case, we know that we have attempted to be forthright in our disclosures beforehand. For example, if we have forewarned our Buyer that the chimney is old, and can only be used for gas log fires, then they are not surprised when their chimney inspector states the same. Their own chimney inspector is likely to provide them an expensive bid to restore or even re-build the chimney so that it could be a wood burning fireplace, as well as a lesser bid for maintenance work to keep the old chimney in its current state of only being able to be used for gas log fires. The difference in these bids can be $10,000 to $20,000 or more. Let's play out the three ways a Buyer can respond.

The "fair" Buyer acknowledges that this is not new information and may request the relatively small amount for the maintenance of the chimney. To this I recommend the Seller agree.

The "unreasonable" Buyer will state that even though they had been forewarned by the Seller about this specific issue, they now want the fireplace updated so that it can used as a wood burning fireplace. This response is usually born out of anxiety or fear rather than any sort of malice. In other words, they want what they were told beforehand that they would not have. To this unreasonable request, I find it best to simply reiterate what was disclosed by the Seller beforehand and re-state the Seller's willingness to remain "fair" by completing or providing a credit for the maintenance of the chimney as a gas log only fireplace. By "fair", I mean that the Seller does not respond emotionally to the Buyer's unreasonable request, but proceeds by responding to the issue. This provides the Buyer the opportunity to respond in kind, and not remain in a state of emotional negotiating. Cooler heads usually prevail and the Seller and Buyer often agree to a fair resolution of the issues raised during the inspection process.

The "unfair" Buyer is simply using the inspection process to renegotiate the purchase contract. Often the Seller cannot differentiate between the unreasonable and the unfair Buyer after the initial response from the Buyer with regards to the inspections. By that, I mean the Seller does not yet have enough information to know whether the Buyer is just reacting emotionally in making unreasonable requests or if they are acting tactically to use the threat of cancelation to get a better deal. A lot can be learned by simply asking the Buyer's representative to further explain the Buyer's request, the reasons for the requests, and the motivation for the requests. For example, a few years ago I represented a Seller and the Buyer was represented by an excellent local agent. The general physical inspection was fairly uneventful so I was surprised when the Buyers requested a credit of $25,000. I called the agent to get more information and she shared that the Buyer felt justified in seeking a credit for a re-roof of the home and garage. I was still surprised, because the Seller had disclosed that he had re-roofed the house within the last ten years with an expensive roofing material. I quickly scheduled a roof inspection with a roofer that I trust. That roofer completed an inspection and stated, "I wish I had this roof on my house. This home has a rolled roof under the concrete tile that could stand on its own." Clearly, we know we do not have a roof issue. Either the Buyer was misinformed by their own inspector, or the Buyer was just attempting to re-negotiate.

The Seller was understandably upset by the request. So how do we determine whether the Buyer was being unreasonable or unfair? We issued a Notice to Perform, which informs the Buyer that after a short time frame, usually 2 calendar days after receipt of the notice, the Seller could exercise their right to cancel if the Buyer has not removed their inspection contingency. Whereas the standard purchase contract gives the Buyer the unilateral right to cancel during a contingency period, a Seller has to take the extra step of formally notifying the Buyer that their contingency period has come to an end. Then, the Seller may cancel if the Buyer fails to remove that contingency. The Seller's intent was to clearly state that they were not going to renegotiate for fear of canceling- essentially removing this as a bargaining chip if that was the intent of the Buyer.

We did this in tandem with providing the Buyer's agent a copy of the roof inspection from our roofer. If the Buyer was simply being unreasonable, this inspection would show there was no warrant for their unreasonable request for such a large credit. I also called the agent to attempt to diffuse the situation and propose that perhaps their inspector was incorrect. Again, the Buyer's agent is a very, very good agent. We had a break through when I asked "Do you know and trust your Buyer's roof inspector? Could he simply be in error?" The Buyer's agent admitted that the roofing contractor that she normally would recommend was unavailable and that the she had never worked with the roof inspector that her client had selected. Ah. Now we could have a fruitful conversation about the validity of the differing opinions of the two roofing inspectors. The Buyers called the Seller's roofing contractor directly and then rescinded their request for the $25,000 credit. It would have been easy for both sides to respond emotionally to this issue, but they were able to move forward in a fair manner by focusing on clarifying the physical issue.

I have to admit that it is rarely so clear as one inspector being completely wrong and another being completely right. A more common example would be one roofing contractor stating the roof has 2 to 5 remaining years of "life" while another will say 7 to 10 years.

We have to return again and again to what the Buyer could reasonably expect the physical condition of the property to be through the Seller disclosure, agent disclosure, and their own viewing of the property while they agreed to the purchase contract in comparison to the condition described in the subsequent inspections. If the Seller had indicated that the plumbing was "all new copper" and the inspection found that not to be the case, then the Buyer has a justified expectation to that "all new copper." If the Seller had not represented any upgrades to the plumbing in a home that is obviously older, then the Buyer should have the expectation that the plumbing is indeed older. Then the question becomes whether or not the older plumbing is performing adequately for plumbing of its age. If it is actively leaking, the Buyer may be entitled to the cost of the repair of those leaks, but not for all new plumbing.

To this, a potential Seller may complain, "How am I to know what the Buyer is expecting the condition of my house to be?" Though that is a fair question, it is not the most fruitful on which to focus. It is better for the Seller's agent to help the Seller answer "What will the Buyer expect to find during the inspection contingency?" In answering this question prior to marketing the property, the Seller will be best prepared.

Inspection surprises can happen, though. There are times when a significant issue does manifest during the Buyer's inspections and is a surprise to both the Seller and the Buyer. No matter what the issue, it must first be clearly defined before the remedy can be quantified. Stated simply: What is the problem and how much will it cost to fix it?

That first step of defining the issue is absolutely necessary for the Seller and the Buyer to be on the same page. For example, as I mentioned early on, the discovery of a problem with the foundation is typically highly sensitive. It is easy for a Buyer to hear that that there is a "problem with the foundation" and interpret that as "the home is not safe and requires a new foundation." Just as a mechanic is rarely justified in suggesting your car needs an entirely new engine, a foundation problem rarely requires an entirely new foundation. This is where it is absolutely vital to have reliable and knowledgeable inspectors who can inspect the problem area and clearly describe it to the Buyer and Seller. This is not the time to Google "foundation problem" and call the company at the top of the search queue. Neither is it the time for either side to introduce an inspector that they know will minimize or maximize the issue to favor their own side. Remember that the goal at this point is a clear understanding of the problem for both the Buyer and the Seller. Typically, a good foundation inspection report will include a description of the entire foundation structure as well as a specific description of the problem area or areas. For the type of construction most common in the neighborhoods in which I work, the inspector will state the location of the crack(s), the amount of linear feet of stem wall affected and/or the number of post and piers affected. Now both the Buyer and Seller have the same understanding, scope, or definition of the foundation problem. This is a great starting point on the road to resolution, but that resolution is rarely immediately clear, for there are often different ways to repair the problem with different costs associated. With foundations, can the cracked areas be stabilized with strapping and filling or does that section of the foundation have to be replaced? The difference in cost could be significant.

I know it seems obvious that the Buyer will want the more expensive or "complete" option, whereas the Seller will want the cheaper option. I ask the Seller to consider which option they would complete if they were not selling the house, but were going to continue to live there. This perspective focuses more on a wise solution rather than whether it is the cheaper or more expensive choice. Once that is decided, then the fairness of that solution can be more convincingly demonstrated to the Buyer for their mutual approval. This does mean that there are times when the Seller accepts that there is a significant repair that is required even though they did not know about the problem before it came to light in the Buyer's inspection period. When this is the case, that issue would have to be disclosed to a subsequent Buyer if the current Buyer cancels. If the next Buyer would be unlikely to accept a lesser solution, it is best to move forward with that solution with the current Buyer. As for the actual completion of the remedy, whenever possible it is advisable for the Seller to provide a credit for the necessary work and let the Buyer perform it after they have completed the purchase.

Yet while we have been resolving the physical inspection contingency, the clock has been running on the other contiguous contingencies as well – namely the appraisal and loan contingencies.

Appraisal

In a typical transaction, the usual Buyer will agree to purchase a home for an agreed upon price, with the condition that the Buyer's Lender appraises the subject property for at least the agreed upon sales price. More often than not, the property does meet this expectation, but what if it does not? If the transaction has an appraisal contingency, the Buyer may unilaterally cancel the purchase contract if the subject property does not appraise. In other words, though a Buyer and a Seller agree to a price, a person that neither the Buyer nor the Seller can talk with or usually ever meet is contracted by the Lender through a third party to make an appointment to see the house, measure the house, review recent sales in the same neighborhood, and then produce a written appraisal report. It is sobering to acknowledge that the Buyer has the right to cancel escrow based upon a written report by a stranger who is suddenly introduced into the sales process.

The default time frame for the appraisal contingency on the standard CAR purchase contract is 17 days. Though I believe in reducing the contingency period as much as possible, if a Seller agrees to an appraisal contingency, it is difficult to remove that contingency in less than 14 days. After the last rise and fall cycle of the residential real estate market that ended in 2007, Lenders have had to change how they obtain an appraisal. They used to be able to directly contact an appraiser on their own approved list and start the appraisal process. The new regulation sought to mitigate interaction between the Lender and the Appraiser, insulating that appraiser from Lender influence as to their value determination of a given property and retaining their purpose as a "check" in this check and balance system. Now Lenders submit a request via a "neutral" third party from which an appraiser is selected from a pool of appraisers.

All this to say- there is a process for the ordering of an appraisal as well as the submission of that eventual appraisal back to the lender that does unfortunately take time. This is an easy place in the management of a transaction for time to be wasted. The listing agent needs to monitor the Buyer's Lender to make sure that they are aware of the agreed upon contractual deadlines and are acting productively to meet those deadlines.

It behooves the Seller and their agent to understand what an appraiser actually does, because their job has changed dramatically in the last few years. With all of the changes in Lending during and after the last recession, the workload placed on appraisers has increased, but their pay has generally decreased. It is a common misconception that an appraiser will independently determine the market value of a given property. If that were true, it would be quite a coincidence for their objective evaluation of a home to exactly match the negotiated purchase price to which a Buyer and Seller agreed. Yet, in practice the vast majority of appraisals "come in at" the exact price that the Buyer and Seller have also agreed to. Why? Because they are not attempting to independently determine the market value of the subject property. Rather, they are given a copy of the agreed upon purchase contract with the order for the appraisal. Their job is to effectively ratify the value that a Buyer and Seller have agreed to on behalf of the chosen Lender.

Typically, the Lender has agreed to lend a given percentage of the price of a property, like 50%, 75%, or most commonly 80%. With the appraisal, the Lender is establishing 80% of what price. The loan product being generated has pricing that is linked to not only the credit worthiness of the Buyer/Borrower, but also to what percentage of the value they are lending. If their percentage is higher, their risk is higher and the interest rate offered to the Buyer is higher. Therefore, the appraisal is simply ratifying that there is a demonstrable argument for the value the Buyer and Seller have agreed to for the subject property by showing that like kind properties within a radius of proximity have recently sold for similar prices.

The listing agent's job includes assisting the appraiser in ratifying the agreed upon sales price and getting the appraisal contingency removed. This can be accomplished in a few easy steps. The first is to be flexible when the appraiser calls to make an appointment to see the property. This sounds so obvious as to be overlooked, but it's an essential step. My mantra- make it easy for the appraiser to complete her/his/their job. Once an appraiser receives an order, they have less than a week to make the appointment to walk the property, physically measure the property and inquire as to the physical details of the property, review the recent sales and listings in that given neighborhood, select the relevant "comparables", research and drive by those comparables, and produce a report that is several pages in length. To make a living, appraisers need to complete several every week and can be driving significant distances to do so. Therefore, the listing agent has to be flexible when they call and say, "Can we meet this Thursday at 11am?" Unless it really is a hardship for the Seller (not the agent), the answer should be, "Sure, see you there at that time."

Once the appointment is made, treat it like any other showing. The home should be in showing shape and the Owner should not be present. Prior to that appointment, I always prepare a package for the appraiser that contains the following: a brochure and MLS print out of the subject property, sold comparables that support the sales price of the subject property, active and pending sales that support the sales price as well, and my card so that if they have a question they can reach me quickly and easily. The comparables provided should fall within what is usable by an appraiser- sold within the last six months and bracketed below, at, and above the sales price of the subject property. All this is just to assist the appraiser in completing their report in a timely manner so that they can ratify the price and we can proceed to the removal of that contingency.

Remember that like everyone else, appraisers have a variety of personalities. Some like talking and are thankful for hearing additional details of the property while others would rather not be spoken to. It is their job to do in the manner in which they choose to do it. Be willing to answer questions and assist them as they require.

Side note- listing agents get calls all the time from appraisers completing appraisals on other properties in which they are using that agent's past sale as a comparable. They usually have a quick question to clarify information about that sale or sales that they need to complete their report. For me, yes, that appraisal has nothing to do with me, but I return that call and answer their question. Why? Because when they call other agents while they are completing an appraisal for one of my sales, I hope the same of other agents.

Most of the time the appraisal will "come in at" the sales price. The Buyer removes their appraisal contingency and we progress. But what about when the appraiser produces an appraisal at a price lower than the agreed upon price of the purchase contract? This can happen and when it does it should not be a surprise to the listing agent. During a negotiation, the listing agent should be aware when the purchase price being negotiated is going to be above what can be substantiated by an appraiser. This is more likely in a multiple offer situation where several Buyers are vying for the same property. As mentioned previously, there are instances when Buyers are tired of competing for homes and not getting them. In a market that is going up, there are times when an astute Buyer is willing to pay more than market value for a home in order to secure that property. Taking a long-term view, a Buyer can decide to pay a future value for a property knowing that they intend to live in the property for several years. In other words, they may think it is better to pay next year's price for a home they love now.

When the negotiations are leading to a sales price that will be challenging to appraise, the listing agent can attempt to also negotiate with the Buyer to eliminate their appraisal contingency. This is obviously advantageous for the Seller as the Buyer is assuming the risk of the appraisal and will be willing to increase their down payment to make up the short fall if there is one. This is an appropriate concession for a Seller to seek in the right circumstance, but it is not common.

The listing agent and Seller may not be able to have the Buyer remove the appraisal contingency altogether, but a lower limit can be agreed to as well that more clearly quantifies the Buyer's risk. For example, I had a smaller home in a sought-after neighborhood that we placed on the market for $739,000. When we completed our pre-marketing preparations and placed it on the market, we quickly received 8 offers with the eventual winning bid being at $785,000. I did feel that the property would not appraise for that price, but I did think it would appraise for $760,000. Instead of asking the Buyer to assume all of the risk of the appraisal, we agreed to amend the appraisal contingency so that it only had to appraise for $760,000. What is at stake for the selected Buyer with 20% down? If the property appraised for $785,000, their 80% loan at $628,000, their down payment remained at 20%, or $157,000. If the property appraised for $760,000, their 80% loan at $608,000, their down payment increased to 23%, or $177,000. If the property appraised for $739,000, their 80% loan at $591,200, their down payment increased to 25%, or $193,800. The winning Buyer was able to accept this risk. The appraisal came in at $765,000 and they were able to increase their down payment within the expected range.

Comparatively, what happens if you have an appraisal contingency and the appraisal comes in at a price lower than the agreed upon sales price? There are really only three possibilities at this point: the Buyer can cancel; the Buyer can remove the contingency and proceed; or the Buyer and Seller negotiate a lower sales price.

The first possibility is that the Buyer chooses to cancel the transaction. Again, the appraisal contingency gives the Buyer the right to unilaterally cancel escrow if the appraisal is not equal to or greater than the agreed upon purchase price. If the Buyer has become unsure of their decision to purchase the subject property, an appraisal report that is lower than the sales price can be enough for a Buyer to choose to back out of the transaction. Before this step is taken, the listing agent can review the appraisal and attempt to correct any errors that have been made by the appraiser and/or suggest other comparables for the appraiser to consider. Most Lenders will encourage this effort, but I have never witnessed an appraiser actually agreeing to alter his/her appraisal report. The goal of this extra effort is to provide the Buyer with a substantive argument for the agreed upon purchase price. This can lead to the second possible outcome- the Buyer removes the appraisal contingency and proceeds to closing by increasing their down payment.

Lastly, the Buyer and Seller can negotiate the sales price again in light of the appraisal report not ratifying the agreed upon sales price. Like all negotiations, this can lead to a compromise- lowering of the sales price by X number of dollars all the way down to the appraised value. As with the inspection issues, the Seller should consider whether this same issue will repeat itself with a subsequent Buyer if the current Buyer backs out. If the Seller's agent can demonstrate that the agreed upon sales price can be supported with relevant comparables, then the risk is less if the current Buyer does cancel.

Last year I represented a property that had multiple offers and sold for $1,320,000, which was $31,000 over the asking price. The appraiser for the chosen Buyer appraised the property for $60,000 under the sales price. The Buyers stated that they would cancel if the Seller did not lower the sales price by $40,000. I reviewed the appraisal report with the Seller extensively. I composed a detailed critique of the appraisal report for the Lender, Buyer, and Seller. Even though the appraiser predictively did not agree to alter his report, the Seller felt there was a substantive argument for the original agreed upon asking price. The Seller rejected the Buyer's demand, let them cancel, and proceeded with the back-up Buyer at $31,000 over the asking price. The Seller accepted the risk of letting the first Buyer cancel because he felt he understood the appraisal issues. That back up Buyer's appraiser ratified that higher sales price and we closed escrow at that higher price.

I cannot stress enough the need for the Seller to know ahead of time if there is going to be a potential appraisal problem. This is yet another crucial part of the listing agent's job on behalf of the Seller. As stated before when we were considering the value of the property prior to placing it on the market, the listing agent has to do so much more than guess at a value and asking price. Recently I marketed a home for $1,850,000. Prior to marketing, I consulted with that Seller regarding the market value of their home. My conclusion was that it would sell for significantly more than what it would likely appraise for during escrow. Knowing this ahead of time, the Seller selected a Buyer that could move forward without an appraisal contingency. In that case, the appraisal came in at $1,700,000 while the home sold for full price at $1,850,000. Selling that property meant not only getting the highest price possible for the Seller in the original negotiations with the Buyer(s), but also shepherding that highest possible price through the inspection and appraisal process. Once those two contingencies are removed, usually the only one left is the loan contingency.

Loans

As with the inspection and appraisal contingencies, the work for the Seller on the loan contingency is almost all done prior to execution of the purchase contract. Verifying that the proposed Buyer is actually qualified for the loan they are proposing is absolutely mandatory by the listing agent on behalf of the Seller. This is done by interviewing the proposed Buyer's Lender about the "approval" process they have completed on behalf of the proposed Buyer. I know we discussed this before in the section about "A" Buyers, but it bears repeating. The listing agent has to know whether the proposed Buyer can actually obtain the loan they are proposing. This is more than reviewing a "pre-approval" letter. It involves vetting the Lender, and then making sure the Lender can substantiate their pre-approval.

Since this work was done by the listing agent prior and during the negotiation of the contract, the task in escrow is to manage the loan contingency. In this instance, manage is a nice word for what looks more like pestering. Lenders are busy and good Lenders are even busier. The Seller's agent's job during the loan contingency is to make sure the Lender stays on track with the Buyer's loan. Without regular check-ins with the Lender, it is too easy for the underwriting process to drag on and cause delays in escrow. It is best to call the Lender with specific questions as the process proceeds. For example, near the beginning of escrow I am calling to make sure the appraisal has been ordered. Once the appraiser has been to the property, I check in with the Lender asking if the appraisal report been submitted to the underwriter. Once that is completed, I call to inquire if the underwriter has reviewed the file and issued the pre-doc and pre-funding conditions and, if so, are there any with which I can be of assistance.

While checking with the Lender directly, it is also important to stay in touch with the Buyer's Agent. When the loan contingency is scheduled to be removed I send the form to the Buyer's Agent and ask them to have it executed by the Buyer and returned to me. If there is hesitancy to remove the loan contingency by the Buyer, I know there is an outstanding issue that needs to be resolved, either with the loan or some other issue that has not been revealed. Since the Loan Contingency is typically the last contingency to be removed by the Buyer, it can feel like the point of no return for the Buyer. Once they remove their final contingency, the Buyer is placing their security deposit at risk if they are unable to close.

Often the Buyer believes the loan contingency remains in place until their Lender informs them that their loan has been fully approved by the underwriter, but this is not true. The loan contingency is a period of time in which the Buyer retains the right to cancel escrow if they believe they are unable to obtain the loan specified in the purchase contract. In other words, it is a period of time in which the Seller bears the risk of the Buyer canceling. In this agreed upon time period the Buyer is to work diligently with their Lender so they are prepared to surrender their right to unilaterally cancel the contract at the agreed upon expiration of that time frame. The listing agent needs to be persistent in requesting that the Buyer remove their contingencies as scheduled in the agreed upon sales contract.

Once the loan and all other contingencies are removed, the Seller can "feel" like they have a deal and make plans to complete the agreed upon repairs if applicable, pack, and prepare to move. This means there is a lot to do in a limited amount of time. The relief in this time frame is that the home no longer needs to be in showing shape. A Seller is wise to consider this time frame back when they are negotiating the purchase contract. Often a Seller will want to close escrow in 30 days, thinking they will have a month to pack and move. In reality, when the contingency period is concluded, the Seller is left with less than two weeks to be ready to close escrow and move. That is why is it so important for the Seller to actually look at the calendar prior to committing to a closing date and be comfortable with the time frame the Seller will have after the contingencies are removed in which to accomplish their move.

There is another less common contingency that is worth mentioning before we conclude this *End* period of the selling process, and that is the contingency to sell or a "Contingent Sale." A Seller can receive an offer from a potential Buyer that includes the contingency of selling their (the Buyer's) current home. From the Buyer's perspective this is an ideal situation; they have found a home they would like to purchase, if only that Seller will give them the time to sell their current property. It is an entirely different story from the Seller's perspective. If the Seller agrees, then the sale of the Seller's property is entirely dependent upon another transaction in which the Seller has absolutely no involvement or control. This means the Seller will have taken their home off the market in hopes that a theoretical sale of another property takes place in some sort of agreed upon timely manner. Why would a Seller ever agree to bear this much risk?

It is interesting to me how many of these types of offers I actually see. Even more interesting is how often a Seller is tempted to consider them. Whether it is a multiple offer situation or just a single offer, this type of "contingent offer" can appear quite enticing for the unaware Seller with a very attractive offering price. Each time it is important to review again what a contingency actually is. A contingency is a condition- if a certain thing occurs, then the next step of the agreement will happen. We have discussed at length the importance of the Seller preparing for each of these contingencies. In preparation of the inspection contingency, the Seller has carefully completed the disclosures and even pre-inspected items that may be of concern to the eventual Buyer. The same diligence of understanding has gone into the appraisal and loan contingencies. Yet now, the Seller is considering a contingency of a property that will also contain these contingencies, but the Seller has no control over the preparation for or lack thereof for these crucial issues of a hoped-for transaction. Do you see now the risk that is really being proposed by a "contingency to sell" Buyer for the Seller? This Buyer is more of a mirage.

It is only rarely that a Seller should consider it best to assume this level of risk for a hoped for transaction. It is usually best to convey to that Buyer that the Seller will be interested if that Buyer is able first sell the property that they need to in order to be able to make a subsequent purchase. As with most rules, there are exceptions. A good example took place recently.

My Seller went on the market and received a few offers. Being a multiple offer situation, the Seller responded to all of the Buyers with an over asking Multiple Counter Offer. When the Buyers responded there was an appreciable price difference between the Buyer at the highest price and the other Buyers. That highest Buyer was contingent upon the sale of their current property. I explained the risks associated with this type of offer but the Seller was still interested in the Buyer. Though I did not represent this Buyer, I had met him and his family at the Open House. They did seem a very good match, with the property's strengths being the features that they were most looking for in a home. The Seller asked me to attempt to find out more about the Buyer and the property they needed to sell. I was direct with their agent stating that the Seller could not consider their offer unless I could determine the viability of the proposed sale of their current home. To do so I would need to tour their property and complete a market analysis of their property. They and their agent cooperated immediately.

Once I completed my analysis of their home, I asked to meet with them and their agent. I presented my opinion of value and even shared the listing price range in which they would need to be to sell in a timely manner. I also asked if they would consider my input into the actual presentation of the home. Again, they and their agent agreed and we completed a room by room assessment of the needed changes to each room as well as the grounds. They committed to completing those preparations, the pricing range I suggested, and the timeframe in which to be on the market. I had also inquired about their disclosures and the condition of their current home. With all of this information, I was able to state to my client that these Buyers would have their current home in escrow within 15 days of going on the market. Weighing all of their offers and they varying degrees of risk, my client considered the risk worth taking and moved forward with this "contingent" Buyer. The Buyer's and their agent's transparency and willingness to take effective action within the guidelines provided by the Seller in a timely manner converted this theoretical Buyer into a real candidate Buyer. Both escrows closed successfully. Though this situation proved a success, it was a very rare exception to the rule that "contingent offers" are unduly risky for a Seller to consider.

Close of Escrow and Moving

Now back to moving forward after the removal of all contingencies. This last step of the transaction may require the most maturity for it is not an easy time. The anxiety of the transaction and the stress of the impending move can sometimes get the best of people, but do not let it be so with you. It is here at the end when a smooth hand off to the Buyer helps avoid an entire host of future problems. I have witnessed the ill will created by a Seller leaving a mess behind after they have moved out. In one case, not only was there a great deal of trash left behind by the Seller throughout the house, attic, garage, and driveway, but also an old dog was left in the rear yard.

The Buyer was understandably upset and threatened a lawsuit. Though amends were quickly made, this is just the type of exit that invites future lawsuits over issues that would not have been escalated to that level if the Seller had only turned over the property in a respectful manner.

The first opportunity to do this is during the Buyer's final walk through. Most contracts give the Buyer the right to a final non-contingent walk through in the last days prior to closing. This provides the Buyer the opportunity to verify that the Seller has maintained the property in the condition in which it was when the purchase contract was agreed to, i.e. the pool has not turned green, the landscaping has not been neglected, and whatever agreed upon repairs have been completed. The listing agent can set the correct tone for this walk through by arranging this at a time that works for both the Buyer and the Seller. At this brief meeting, the listing agent should invite the Buyer to verify that any agreed upon repairs have indeed been completed. It is very helpful for the listing agent to provide the Buyer and their agent copies of receipts for said work. If the Seller is present, the listing agent can then invite the Buyer to ask the Seller any questions they may have about the house. This is not an inspection so the questions are more along the lines of "What day to the trash barrels go out in this neighborhood?" The Seller can in turn share some helpful details of the property that they have learned while living there. A casual, friendly, yet brief conversation is more than appropriate between the Buyer and the Seller, for this transaction is after all about a home. This can be a great time of handshakes and sincere good wishes. Arrangements for keys are planned for after the close of escrow.

Once this is done, the Buyer is typically busy executing loan documents and wiring funds to escrow. The listing agent has to monitor these last few days for the Seller very closely. If something arises that could cause the Lender to even delay the funding of their loan one day, it can negatively affect the Seller. The worst case scenario is for the Seller to move out of the property as per the timeframe of the purchase contract, but the escrow closing is delayed for any number of reasons. Whenever possible, it is less risky for the Seller to have the right to remain in the property for a couple of days after the close of escrow. With this right, the Seller can know that escrow is closed prior to actually moving out of the property. As stated earlier, it is all too easy for the Lender to have some sort of issue that delays the close of escrow a few days. Though this may not seem important to the Lender, it can cause a great deal of inconvenience for the Buyer and Seller who have scheduled their moving companies, utilities, mail, babysitters, and a whole host of other details necessary when moving. The right to remain for a couple of days after escrow also gives the Seller a chance to make sure the property is left in a clean condition. It's not only a "nice" thing to do, but a good business decision to hand off the property well to the Buyer.

Chapter
9

Conclusion

I will never forget when my wife and I were told by our doctor that our daughter had a tumor in the growth plate of her jaw. The slight asymmetry of her angelic face would turn warped if left unchecked, and eventually destroy her jaw. Not only one but two painful surgeries were proposed, the first to remove the tumor, and the second to re-structure her jaw once she was fully grown. Second and third opinions only confirmed the diagnosis and the proposed surgical remedies. The best decision was to proceed. Our daughter endured the first surgery as well as the painful years of waiting through high school before an even more painful second surgery the summer before she left for college. There is so much in this time that is my daughter's own private story to tell, but we are all so thankful for the doctor that guided us through the several years' medical remedy. That space in which my wife and I thought and prayed about the right course of action for our daughter with the counsel of the doctor was truly sacred.

I marvel still today how that doctor took the time to prepare us to make such a difficult decision. He deciphered x-rays and CT scans for us, taught us about the growth of the teenage jaw-bone, and explained the risks of the various facial nerves that were in close proximity of the affected area. He even made 3D models of her jaw to help synthesize all the bewildering data into terms that we could comprehend. He quite literally taught us how to make the best decision possible in a difficult medical situation. The percentage of time he spent actually in surgery with our daughter was quite small in comparison to the time he spent preparing us all for those surgeries and coaching us through both of the painful recoveries. He invested his time with us.

As we have walked together through the evaluation of a home, the preparation of that property prior to placing it on the market, and the actual sales process through to closing, we have witnessed the large investment of time that is required of the listing agent in the process of selling a home. Do you now see the actual job of the listing agent? That role is to bring the right questions to the homeowner at the right time in the process in order to provide that Seller with the optimal environment in which to make all of the necessary decisions in their most optimal sequence. It is this optimal environment, this three-dimensional space entered by the agent, this functional mission control room where the principals make their critical decisions, that is the sacred ground.

The fiduciary responsibility is the agent's invitation to enter reverently into that space in which our clients seek to make good decisions about their homes. The cost to the agent is time. And it is this time element that will result in the coming striations in the field of residential real estate. Earlier in this book I defined the three historical levels of agents that have traditionally operated under the same agreement of assisting a client with the sale of their home for some percentage of the sales price, historically between 5 and 6%.

No longer will the mere expeditor of real estate transactions survive. There are just too many online data sources and online brokerages that can replace the expeditor of a transaction while providing significant savings for the principal- those do it yourself Buyers and Sellers that do not feel the need for a real estate agent in their real estate decision process. It is these real estate agents, a relatively small minority, that provide no real beneficial context for all of the details that require attention in a transaction, but still want to be paid as if they do. This subset of agents is already being replaced by online real estate sites and platforms such as Redfin and Rex that offer a significant lowering of the traditional commission percentages.

The evolving electronic real estate market place will also put a squeeze on the second tier of agents. By second tier, I am not referring to how financially successful they are. This second tier perceives the real estate industry as a gold mine and they are quite willing to work diligently as they dig to get at those rich veins of gold. This tier has some brilliant and industrious players. It is by the sweat of their brows that they take those daily risks in the real estate mine, and some of them are wildly successful. By the gold standard, many are elite. They adhere to the code of ethics for Realtors and consider their fiduciary responsibility as a firm line that is not to be crossed. Yet, it is this merely two-dimensional view of the fiduciary responsibility that may prove to be their Achilles heel. As artificial intelligence is introduced to the electronic real estate capabilities, what then will these agents be offering that cannot be duplicated at a cheaper and more efficient rate? Intentional time is required to add that third necessary dimension to build out the fiduciary space in which the client can be best served. And time is the most valuable of commodities. Because of time we must come to terms with its limit.

This past year I assisted my clients in thirty-two real estate transactions. I believe this is about 75 to 80% of what I have the capacity to do in a given year while maintaining the quality of work to which I am committed for each client as well as being responsible to the other commitments in my life. I am certainly not the measure of production capacity for real estate agents. There are agents with vastly greater capacity that can maintain the quality of their work while completing many more transactions; but they all do have their limits. Each of us has a limit beyond which the quality of our work will degrade.

As with most sales jobs, the measuring device for the success of an agent is a comparison of the volume of sales completed by that agent. The logic is obvious. Those that make more money at a job must be those that are better at that job – as it is a survival of the fittest competition. There is obvious merit to this as those who do the most amount of business become the most experienced. By this logic, we should have chosen our daughter's surgeon based upon who has completed the most similar surgeries. Though experience was an important factor, it was more about who would bring all of their experience, skill, and care to bear on this one single patient- our precious daughter. It was ultimately a decision of quality rather than quantity.

Knowing myself, I seek to complete 30 to 40 transactions a year in order to maintain my quality of performance at that level of work load. For some that number might be 150, and for still others it may be 15. The goal is not comparison to one another, but to oneself. Contentment and ambition do not have to be juxtaposed, but rather a decision of the quality of work and the quality of life made by each agent that is dedicated to doing this job well on their client's behalf.

The current popular models for dealing with limits can be summed up as "do a better job of delegating." For those who manage and coach real estate agents, they know that only about 10% of agents actually do enough transactions that this idea of capacity and limits is even relevant. The average real estate agent has plenty of time to do their job very well for each client. The issue is that a large share of transactions is completed by those relatively few agents that make up the top producing agents. Becoming one of these top agents is the goal of most of the other agents in their office. While those top producing agents are moving as quickly as possible as though their hair is on fire, the majority of the agents have more than enough time and not enough transactions to fill that time.

Agents with too much time are always encouraged to "do more, do more, do more," while those who are actually doing more are still encouraged to keep "doing more" because that is what got them there in the first place. How? Through delegation. Let's say an agent of great capacity is completing 100 transactions a year and is doing a great job for her clients. This agent will be asked to define those activities she is doing in each transaction that take time, but are not "essential." This is a valuable time management question which can both be effective and wise. The problem today is that so many "essential" tasks of a productive agent are being re-defined as "non-essential" and then delegated to increase production, subsequently diluting the quality of the work being done.

All real estate agents are aware of "those" agents in their area that disappear once a contract is negotiated and escrow has been opened. The critical process of disclosures, inspections, appraisals are "handled" by a parade of assistants and "team members" that are not prepared nor qualified to be the nuanced steward of the task delegated to them. Why? Because that agent is more dedicated to increasing the number of transactions than the quality of the transaction. They are in charge at mission control, and their clients are just passengers that they launch, leaving the trajectory and landing to gravity. Their sale numbers may increase for a time, but with a very predictable trail of damaged clients behind. They become mere expeditors of real estate transactions.

It is this model that can be reproduced by a computer algorithm that can complete real estate transactions. Supplying data of the inventory, filling out forms, and completing a real estate transaction is not that difficult. But to assist someone in the making of a good real estate decision does indeed take a significant amount of time, experience, and effort on someone else's behalf. I do not see a shortcut for doing this job well.

Perhaps there is an opportunity for more clarity in the residential real estate market. Since online real estate platforms and their algorithms can at best mimic the expediting agent, let's redefine this type of representation as something other than agency that is de-coupled from the pretension of attempting to satisfy the fiduciary responsibility of true agency. Both the electronic data platform and its servicers could assist a Buyer and a Seller that prefers their own data analysis and market understanding at a significant commission savings that is not even based on a percentage, but is more akin to a time and materials contractor. This would be a much more transparent decision for the Buyer/Seller and more accurately reflect the current reality of the residential market where a rather large number of agents are being paid large commissions while not satisfying their fiduciary responsibilities.

I am so thankful for the many agents I have met over the past 30 years that are really good at their jobs. It is this significant minority that gives me confidence that there will continue to be quality agents available for those Buyers and Sellers that are fortunate enough to work with them. This group will always refine their skills and be open to incorporating technological advances that help them to better serve their clients.

On a more macro-scale, I am concerned about my own sales industry's treatment of this sacred space. There are those within it who are attempting to manipulate that sacred space for their own gain. The purchase and sale of a home is a point where a lot of dollars are being spent- not only agent fees, but escrow, title, lender, insurance, contractors, movers, home furnishings, home security, and a host of others. I listened to the owner of a large real estate company discussing with his management team how they could best leverage their "trusted position at the center of real estate transactions" to earn a greater share of all those other dollars. That company was sold soon after for a premium to an even larger real estate company, which these many years later, inspired the title of this book. The irony is obvious; as more real estate companies seek to leverage their "trusted" position with their clients, the less trust will be developed. The sacred is not "priceless" because it has such a high market value. It is sacred because it has a price that the market is unable to pay.

A wise friend of mine is keen to say "The main thing, is to keep the main thing, the main thing." In the real estate business that "main thing" is the principal, the client, the Seller, the Buyer. The job of the agent is always "What is best for the client?" and not "What is the best way to make more money from the client?" There are times when the best decision for the principal is not to proceed with a given purchase or sale. Unless an agent and their company are willing to support that when it is the best decision, they are not committed to their fiduciary responsibility to their client. And it is this type of whole hearted embrace of the fiduciary responsibility that may make the role of the residential real estate expert indispensable to the home Seller and home Buyer in the near term and far-off marketplace.

About the Author

It's an odd path that led Craig to real estate. Raised as the youngest child of Norwegian immigrant parents, hard work was prized in their home, but certainly not in any fashion that drew attention to oneself. His undergraduate degree is in Chemistry from UC Irvine, but his love of science did not match his rather average aptitude for it. He then attended grad school at Fuller Seminary, showing a bit more aptitude, but clearly not made for ministry as a profession. It was the love of a girl that eventually led him to real estate. He told this girl that he loved her when they were in the 8th grade together, but it would be more than ten years before she decided she loved him as well. As her family was a second-generation real estate family, he jumped into the real estate pool to swim, or die trying back in 1988.

His favorite living authors are Neal Stephenson and NT Wright, but he assumes neither would be pleased to hear it. He is an ardent fan of his three grown children. And he is sure he has better friends than he deserves.

CPSIA information can be obtained
at www.ICGtesting.com
Printed in the USA
JSHW081558290323
39644JS00003B/354